Revelation

for You and Me

John Iles

Published and printed by Lulu.com

Copyright © John Arthur Iles 2018

All rights reserved. No part of this publication may be reproduced, stored in a retrieval system, or transmitted, in any form or by any means, electronic, mechanical, photocopying, recording or otherwise, without prior permission of the publisher.

Scripture quotations are from the Holy Bible, English Standard Version, published by HarperCollins Publishers © 2001 by Crossway Bibles, a division of Good News Publishers. Used by permission. All rights reserved.

Cover illustration by Becky Iles

First published 2018

British Library Cataloguing in Publication Data

A catalogue record for this book is available from the British Library.

ISBN: 978-0-244-08686-2

Contents

Chapter	Passage	Page
1. Everything Under Control	Rev.1:1-20	1
2. Trouble in the Church	Rev.2:1 to 3:22	9
3. Heaven's Perspective	Rev.4:1 to 5:14	22
4. The Seals	Matthew 24	
	Rev.6:1 to 7:17	32
5. Trumpets and Bowls	Rev.8:1 to 9:21	
	Rev.11:15-19	
	Rev.15:1 to 16:21	42
6. Faithfulness and Vindication	Rev.10:1 to 11:14	53
7. Spiritual Warfare	Rev.12:1 to 13:18	63
8. Harvest Time	Rev.14:1-20	74
9. The End of Human Opposition	Rev.17:1 to 19:5	81
10. Celebrations	Rev.19:1-21	91
11. Thrones and Dominions	Rev.20:1-15	98
12. For the Glory of God	Rev.21:1 to 22:21	105

1. Everything Under Control
Revelation 1:1-20
Apocalypse

As the first word of this book in Greek states, this book is an apocalypse. That is, it is a revelation by God of things which otherwise we could not possibly know.

There are some important differences between Revelation and other apocalyptic writings. It is usual in them to provide explanations of the visions. But most of the visions in Revelation are shown without any explanation. The purpose of the visions is not so that a particular historical event can be identified with a particular vision in order that the next event can be predicted. It is rather to tell of the kind of thing that will happen at different times. It is to help the Christian to see historical events from God's point of view and to adopt an appropriate attitude towards them.

The book is not simply apocalyptic. It does not only foretell cataclysmic events which will destroy the present order to clear the way for a completely new beginning. The present is evidently worth dealing with and putting to rights. This is shown by the fact that the moral and spiritual needs of the Church are directly addressed in chapters 2 and 3.

The present is not shown to be a total disaster. In spite of the apparently unrestricted influence the evil one exerts over the world rulers, and in spite of the suffering experienced by the Church in consequence, God is in control. Victory will come through suffering. That is the path Jesus Christ trod (1:17-18) and those who would follow Him must tread it too.

This revelation is unique in that it is "the revelation of Jesus Christ" (1:1). It has been given to Him by God.

It is His to tell. This He does by telling it to John with instructions to write what he is shown and pass it on to the Church (1:11).

It is His to do. He is the one who sets in motion the phases and features of God's plan of judgment and salvation.

It is His in that He is the central figure of this revelation. The spotlight is on Him. That is why the first vision of the book is of the risen Lord Jesus Christ (1:9-20), and the final words of prophecy are His, "Surely I am coming soon." (22:20)

Since the out-workings of history are in His hands, it is good for Christians to be reminded of what sort of person He is.

The Faithful Witness

"Witness" (1:5) is from the Greek word "martyr". Today when we think of martyrs we immediately think of their deaths. But in New Testament times the emphasis was on the fact that they were faithful to what they believed and refused to recant.

For Jesus Christ it was more than simply believing in something or someone and being faithful to those beliefs. He was faithful to Himself, to who He is.

He is the Word of God (John 1:1). This does not mean simply an arrangement of letters which may be written or spoken. The Word of God is God at work. God speaks with purpose. At creation God said, "Let there be light" and light came into being. That continued throughout the creation account; everything was made through God giving a command and it was done (Gen.1:3-27; John 1:3). The Word of God never fails to achieve what God intends (Isa.55:10-11).

In Jesus the Word of God became a man (John 1:14). In doing so He showed us what the invisible God is like (John 1:18). Jesus did not only claim to speak the truth, He said, "I am the truth" (John 14:6). So that in everything He was and said and did, He faithfully showed God to the world. This was in spite of the fact that He knew that the religious leaders would kill Him (Mark 8:31) for what He said (John 5:18) and did (Mark 3:1-6).

The fact that He is faithful is vitally important, especially for Christians who are suffering persecution. He calls them to be faithful (Rev.2:10). He doesn't just call them. He is faithful in every way and will guard and keep them from all evil (2 Thess.3:3).

The Firstborn of the Dead

Jesus came to die (Mark 10:45). He laid down His life deliberately, always intending to rise again (John 10:17). He could do that because He is "the living one" (Rev.1:18), the one who has
"life in Himself" (John 5:26).

The statement that He is "the firstborn of the dead" indicates that He is one of many who will rise (cf. Rom.8:29). Just as all die because of Adam's sin so Jesus made resurrection possible for others by His sinless life, His obedient death and His resurrection (1 Cor.15:21-22).

But the resurrection life is not something that He gives that is separate from Himself. He said, "I am the resurrection and the life" (John 11:25). To enjoy the resurrection life, we need Him.

Those who accept His death as being in their place, as Him dying for their disobedience to God, are "united with Him" in His death (Rom.6:5). It is as if when Christ died they died and all punishment due was borne, all debt was paid. All such believers will be "united with Him in a resurrection like His" – they too will be raised again on the last day (John 6:40). Those who believe in Him will live even though they die (John 11:25-26).

Jesus has the "keys of Death and Hades" (Rev.1:18). He can and will set free those who are subject to death and the fear of it (Heb.2:15). So, for the believer, all fear of death is taken away because it is not the end. This was the message the persecuted Church of John's day needed to hear. This is why, down through the centuries, Christians have submitted to death at the hands of their persecutors rather than deny their faith.

The King of Kings

Revelation was probably written during the reign of the Roman emperor Domitian (AD 81 to 96). During that time Christians were experiencing persecution. How organised that was we do not know. It is hard to find evidence of empire-wide persecution of Christians by Domitian.

John, the writer of Revelation (1:1-2), had suffered persecution and had been exiled to the island of Patmos (1:9). In addressing his fellow Christians, he refers to himself as "your brother and partner in the tribulation". Evidently others were suffering too. The Christians in Smyrna were warned about suffering they were about to endure (2:10). One member of the church in Pergamum had already been killed (2:13).

It is worth noting that he was their "brother and partner", not only in tribulation but also in "the kingdom and the patient endurance that are in Jesus". Being united to Christ and in His kingdom will inevitably involve tribulation and require patient endurance. This has been true from the beginning of the Church, even when tribulation has not involved physical abuse or killing. That is why Jesus told His disciples, "In the world you will have tribulation. But take heart, I have overcome the world" (John 16:33).

In Revelation, the power of Rome is represented by a beast with ten horns and seven heads. It is like a leopard, but with feet like a bear's and a mouth like a lion's (13:1-2). A fitting beast for an apocalyptic vision! It receives its power and authority from the dragon, which is Satan (12:9). The whole world bows before the authority of the beast and whatever it decrees stands (13:7-10). It seems that the beast is all-powerful.

But Jesus is "the ruler of kings on earth" (1:5). Probably being "clothed with a long robe and with a golden sash around his chest" (1:13) are indications of His royal status. He bears the name "King of kings and Lord of lords" (19:16), and not one of His enemies can stand against Him (19:15).

He makes war with "a sharp two-edged sword" which comes from His mouth (1:16; 19:15). Since He is the Word of God, it is what He says that will achieve His purposes: all that is evil and opposed to God will be destroyed.

This is the message which the Church needs to hear whenever it is experiencing persecution or opposition, or trouble of any kind.

The Redeemer

Jesus Christ is the one "who loves us" (1:5). In the New Testament loving is not merely a matter of emotions, the way one feels about another person. It is "active concern". To love is to see someone in need and to do whatever is possible to meet that need. So when it is said that Christ loves us, the reasonable question to ask is, "What has He done and what is He doing for us?" The answer is that He sets us free (1:5).

The oldest and best-known story of God setting people free is the one recorded in the book of Exodus, of the Hebrews being set free from slavery in Egypt. God told Moses to tell the people that He would deliver them from slavery (Ex.6:6). He immediately went on to say, "I will **redeem** you." Hundreds of years later God reminded them, "I brought you up from the land of Egypt and **redeemed** you from the house of slavery" (Mic.6:4).

Setting free from slavery is redemption because a price must be paid to secure the release of the slave. A price was paid by the Egyptians in that they suffered through the plagues and especially in the deaths of their firstborn (Ex.11:4-5). A price was paid by the Hebrews in the lamb that had to be killed and its blood smeared on their doorframes so that their firstborn sons would not die but would also be set free (Ex.12:3-13).

We are naturally enslaved in that we all sin, we disobey God's laws. These are set out in their most fundamental form in the Ten Commandments (Ex.20:1-17). Jesus said (Matt.22:37-39) that they are summed up in two commandments: to love God with all the heart, soul and mind (Deut.6:5), and to love one's neighbour as oneself (Lev.19:18). Without any effort, and mostly without thinking about it, we disobey those laws because sin masters us.

Through faith in Christ we are set free from the guilt and punishment of that law-breaking. The price He paid for our redemption is His blood (1:5; Eph.1:7). That is, He bought our freedom by dying in our place as the lamb did for the Hebrew slaves.

Through faith in Christ we are set from the power of sin. He has "made us a kingdom" (1:6). Instead of being slaves we are free citizens of the Kingdom of God, living under His rule. He has made us "priests to His God and Father". More and more, as He changes our hearts, we become those who serve God and worship Him by the way we live (Rom.6:22; Rom.12:1-2).

The Alpha and the Omega

These are the first and last letters of the Greek alphabet. The title Alpha and Omega is equivalent to "the first and the last" (22:13).

This is a claim that the LORD, the God of Israel makes for Himself. He does so to make it clear that the gods of the heathen are nothing but idols of wood and stone (Isa.44:6).

In another context He uses the title to show that He is in complete control of creation and all earthly powers (Isa.48:12-

22). He is the One they should fear and obey. He is the One who will rescue them.

The Alpha and the Omega is also equivalent to "the beginning and the end" (22:13). The Alpha and the Omega began everything at creation and will bring everything to the conclusion which He has determined (21:6). He begins a work of salvation in the believer's heart and life and will not leave it unfinished (Phil.1:6).

Christ claims all this for Himself (1:17). He is Immanuel, "God with us" (Matt.1:23). He is the Word of God made flesh (John 1:1, 14). He is one with the Father (John 10:30). With the present and the future in His hands, what does any Christian have to fear? "We can confidently say, 'The Lord is my helper; I will not fear; what can man do to me?'" (Heb.13:6)

The Head of the Church

In "Asia" (1:4), the Turkey of today, there were more than seven churches. In the Bible seven is symbolic of completeness (cf. Gen.2:3). So "the seven churches" are representative of the whole Church of Christ, not only as it existed in John's time but through the centuries.

In the first vision of Revelation the Church is represented by seven lampstands. They are golden because they are precious and sacred to Christ. The risen Christ stands "in the midst" of them. The phrase signifies that He is always there and is always at work on their behalf.

In His right hand He holds seven stars. These represent "the angels of the seven churches" (1:20). Exactly what is meant by "angels" is not clear. Suggested meanings have included guardian angels, the essential spirits of the churches, and the leading elders. Whatever was meant, Christ has these influential beings in His strong right hand. He is the Head of the Church (Eph.4:15-16).

This can be both a comfort and a warning. He is there to guide (2:14-16), to encourage (2:10) and to protect (3:10). He is also there to discipline (2:4-5).

Coming Again

He is coming again (1:7). Then His coming will not be confined to a tiny land in the Middle East, but "every eye shall see Him".

He came the first time to save (Luke 19:10). He will come a second time as judge (Acts 17:30-31). So it will be a time of great dread for "those who pierced Him" (1:7) and for those who, like them, have persisted in their opposition and enmity towards Him.

For those who have believed in Him, accepted Him and followed Him it will be a time of great rejoicing. He will be coming to take them to be with Him forever (John 14:3; 1 Thess.4:13-18). He will save them from the presence of sin and temptation (Heb.9:28). For them there will be no more suffering. Instead they will share in His glory (Rom.8:18).

2. Trouble in the Church

Revelation 2:1 to 3:22

The Whole Church

As has already been noted, there were more than seven churches in the Roman province of Asia. The Book of Acts and the epistles show that there were many other churches in the Roman Empire. In the Bible, seven is the number of completeness.

The seven churches symbolise the whole of the Church of Christ in every place and at all times. That being so, the messages which Christ sent to those seven must be relevant to the whole of His Church. That includes the Church in the twenty-first century, and every local church wherever it may be.

A Personal Response

Each letter is addressed to "the angel" of the particular church. That must mean the one who has overall responsibility for that local church. Whoever is meant by "angel", it is evident from the contents of each letter that the members were intended to hear and obey what Christ had to say.

This is shown by the fact that wherever there is a problem that needs to be put right, Christ calls on individuals to respond. At the end of each letter it is "the one who conquers" who will receive the blessings. Most clearly of all, when Christ is shut outside a church, it is to the one who opens the door that He will enter and with whom He will share a harmonious meal (3:20).

Works

A creed is important because what is believed determines behaviour. In these letters, Christ is mainly concerned with "works", with the behaviour that follows from what is believed. In five of the letters (all seven in the KJV) the message begins with "I know your works". In the letter to Ephesus He commends the church for hating the Nicolaitans' works, not merely their teaching. In many other ways it is made clear that, in these letters, the Lord is chiefly concerned about the way His people behave.

The Person of Christ

Each letter begins with a reminder of who Jesus is, most of them relating back to what John had written in chapter one, especially to the vision he had been given of the risen Lord.

In several of the letters the reminder clearly relates to the message that follows. The One "who holds the seven stars in his right hand, who walks among the seven golden lampstands" (2:1) goes on to say that, if things are not put right, He will "remove [their] lampstand from its place" (2:5). He who "died and came to life" (2:8) is able to promise the faithful of Smyrna that they "will not be hurt by the second death" (2:11). Christ "has the sharp two-edged sword" (2:12) and says of the heretics that He will come "and war against them with the sword of my mouth" (2:16). The One who has "eyes like a flame of fire" (2:18) is the One who "searches mind and heart" (2:23).

The "seven spirits" are referred to in 1:4 as being before God's throne. In the letter to Sardis, Christ says that He has the seven spirits (3:1). The phrase probably refers to the Holy Spirit, and the Lord is saying that He is able to give the Spirit to those who ask (cf. Luke 11:13; Acts 2:32-33). Perhaps the other part of His reminder, that He has the seven stars, is to say that those who have overall responsibility for the church are in special need of the Spirit.

Jesus Christ "has the key of David" (3:7; Isa.22:22). The key of David gives entry into the City of David which is Jerusalem. No doubt here the reference is to entry into the New Jerusalem (21:2). Whatever doors and opportunities are closed to those who are faithful to Jesus Christ, He opens the door of heaven to them and no-one can keep them out (3:8). The promises to "the one who conquers" are all related to that (3:12).

The Lord Jesus is "the beginning of God's creation" (3:14). He is the Alpha and the Omega, the first and the last, the beginning and the end (22:13). He began everything at creation and will bring everything to the conclusion which He has determined (21:6).

The letters were written, wrongs were condemned and warnings were given because He is the One who "loves us" (1:5). At the end of the letters He assures the Church, "Those whom I love, I reprove and discipline" (3:19).

From the fact that all these reminders are given, it is obviously vitally important that the Church should remember who Jesus is. It is because of who He is that He is able to say repeatedly "I know". He knows what is wrong with their behaviour. He knows what He will do to deal with those wrongs. He knows what they are suffering or are about to suffer. He knows the outcome for those who remain faithful to Him.

It goes deeper than that. Whenever a church organisation or a local church has forgotten or denied who the Lord Jesus Christ is, it has, at best, lapsed into mere humanism and ceased to be a true church of Christ.

Patient Endurance

Three of the churches are commended for their "patient endurance" (2:2, 19; 3:10). This was not a stoical gritting of the teeth and putting up with suffering. It meant taking positive action.

It meant being faithful to His name (2:3, 13; 3:8). This was wanting to be associated with Him. It meant not denying that they knew Him as Peter had done when Jesus was arrested (Matt.26:69-75). The Christians of Pergamum had not denied Him even when Antipas had been killed for his faith.

Patient endurance involved keeping Christ's word (3:8, 10). Paul had warned the elders of the church in Ephesus that there would arise in the church "men speaking twisted things, to draw away the disciples after them" (Acts 20:30). This had evidently happened, but the church had tested these "apostles" and found them to be false. Christ commends the church for that (2:2).

The churches in Ephesus (2:2) and Thyatira (2:19) are both commended for patiently continuing to do good works. The works of Ephesus are described as "toil", which describes laborious, painful effort. The works of Thyatira are referred to as "service", which means that they made themselves servants to others. Instead of being deterred by opposition and suffering, the Christians there were actually doing more. The Lord told them, "Your latter works exceed the first" (2:19). Paul wrote to Christians in the neighbouring province of Galatia, "Let us not grow weary of doing good" (Gal.6:9). The churches in Asia may have read that letter.

The temptation to sexual immorality had to be patiently endured. This temptation was obviously strong in Thyatira (2:20) and probably in Pergamum and Ephesus through the teaching of the Nicolaitans and "the teaching of Balaam" (2:14). The temptation had evidently been resisted by the majority of the members of those churches.

The secret of successfully enduring all these things with patience is to not deny His faith (2:13, 19). This means continuing to believe in Him, to trust in His faithfulness however hard things get. Paul wrote, "I can do all things through Christ who strengthens me" (Phil.4:13).

Offending Individuals

Ahab, king of Israel married a foreign princess, Jezebel,

who led him into the worship of Baal (1 Kings 16:31). Her intention was to make Baal worship the national religion. An essential element of Baal worship was the use of cult prostitutes.

Christ may have referred to the woman in the church in Thyatira as Jezebel because she was doing what that queen of Israel had done. She was "teaching and seducing" Christ's servants into idolatry and its associated sexual immorality (2:20).

There was a similar problem in Pergamum. The letter to that church refers to "the teaching of Balaam". When the Israelites were approaching Canaan after their exodus from Egypt, Balak king of Moab summoned the prophet Balaam to curse them. The story is told in Numbers 22 to 24. The LORD God would only allow Balaam to bless His people the Israelites. To earn the money which Balak had promised him, Balaam evidently told the king that the best way to weaken the Israelites was to lead them into Baal worship (Num.25:1-2), that is, into idolatry and sexual immorality. The same thing was happening in Pergamum (2:14).

Nothing is known with any certainty about the Nicolaitans (2:6, 15). It is probable that idolatry and sexual immorality were encouraged by them also.

In Pergamum it was not the whole church that was at fault, only "some" individuals (2:14-15). The error of the church in Thyatira was that they were tolerating Jezebel and what she was doing (2:20). But not all were following her teaching (2:22). In condemning these evils Christ warns that He will come and deal with the offending individuals (2:16, 21-23).

Offending Churches

For Ephesus, Sardis and Laodicea, the warnings are more serious even though the offences appear to be less so. Christ's response would be to deal with the whole church not just with individual offenders.

Sardis was a prosperous city and had been the capital of Croesus, king of Lydia, whose wealth is legendary. It had been built on a very steep hill, apparently immune to attack. When first Cyrus and then Antiochus attacked at night they found the city unguarded and captured it easily. This careless attitude seems to have pervaded the church. It had a good reputation but no real enthusiasm (3:1). As a result, good works were carried out half-heartedly or were begun but never carried through (3:2). Jesus Christ warns the church that he "will come like a thief". Exactly how He would deal with the church is not stated, but He says, "I will come against you" (3:3).

The church in Ephesus had "abandoned the love [they] had at first" (2:4). To begin with their main concern was to live to please God and to be moved by active concern for others. But that love had faded. Concern for doctrinal correctness had taken its place. Christ warns them that He will come and remove their lampstand from its place (2:5). Neither the church nor the city exists today.

However doctrinally correct a church is, when it ceases to be motivated by love for God and for others, it ceases to be relevant and it will die.

Laodicea was a banking centre, had a prosperous textile industry and was famous for the production of a special eye ointment. The church was evidently prosperous too (3:17) and had no sense of any need. They did not realise that although they were materially wealthy, spiritually they were poor, naked and blind (3:17). What they needed could not be obtained in their city but had to be "bought" from their Lord (3:18). Jesus was the only one who could meet their spiritual needs.

Because of their complacent attitude, they were no doubt willing to go along to church meetings and to observe religious rituals, but as to getting into the business of being a 24/7 Christian, they really could not be bothered with that. Christ describes them as being lukewarm, neither cold nor hot (3:16). They were like the tepid water, full of lime, which came from the nearby springs: not hot enough to cleanse, not cool enough to refresh. Jesus said that He would spit them out of His mouth.

Faithful Churches

It is so encouraging to find that Christ finds no fault with two of the seven churches.

Unlike Laodicea, the church in Smyrna knew that they were poor in material things, but Jesus saw that they were spiritually rich (2:9). The only warning He gave them is of imminent persecution through suffering and imprisonment.

The church in Philadelphia was commended for its faithfulness in spite of having "little power" (3:8). Being aware of weakness can be an advantage if the reaction is to depend on God's power (2 Cor.12:7-9). Christ encouraged them to hold fast what they had (3:11).

Remember

If the Church is to benefit from the Lord's rebukes and warnings, there must be a response. In these letters three aspects of the response required are set out.

The first is to remember. The call to the church in Ephesus is "Remember from where you have fallen" (2:5). Jesus used the same word when He foretold the destruction of Jerusalem and said that its inhabitants would "fall by the edge of the sword" (Luke 21:24). He used the same idea when He spoke of the fall of the house built on sand (Matt.7:27). So the church in Ephesus had suffered a catastrophic fall. Remembering their first condition should make them realise that and want to do something about it.

The church in Sardis was called to remember what they

had "received and heard" (3:3). They were to think back to the preaching of the Gospel and the teaching about Christian living to which they had first responded. If they were to "keep it", to set out to trust in Christ alone and to live to please Him, all would be well.

Repent

It is obvious from this that remembering is ineffective unless it is followed by repentance. All five of the churches that have problems are called upon to repent (2:5, 16, 22; 3:3, 19). To repent is not merely to feel remorse, or to be sorry, it is a complete change of mind. Repentance is an about turn, a turning the back upon wrong beliefs and behaviour, and turning to God and His ways. This is not something that Christ will do for the churches, it is something they have to decide to do for themselves.

Conquer

The churches were called to remember and repent. Individuals were called to conquer, to be victors. Every letter draws to a close with the phrase "the one who conquers". This is followed by promises of the blessings the victors will enjoy.

The idea of conquering comes from the games. The Christian life is like running a race. Towards the end of his life Paul wrote that he had finished the race (2 Tim.4:7). It is a marathon rather than a short sprint. It is a race that requires the patient endurance (Heb.12:1) for which three of these churches were commended. They had not always exercised that quality in the right way.

It is a race in which there is no place for the complacency of Laodicea or the half-heartedness of Sardis. Christ appealed to the church in Philadelphia, "Hold fast what you have, so that no-one may seize your crown" (3:11). Paul had the same idea in his mind when he reminded the Christians in Corinth that "in a race all the runners run, but only one receives the prize". He appealed to them to live for Christ with the same dedication as if there would be only one victor (1 Cor.9:24).

Sin weighs the Christian runner down (Heb.12:1). The sexual immorality of Thyatira and the lovelessness of Ephesus must be laid aside. It is the works that are acceptable to Christ that must be kept "to the end" (2:26).

Victors are those who refuse to be side-tracked by the attractions of an easy or a sinful life and remain faithful to the end (Matt.10:24). This will be a constant struggle but it is the one "who remains steadfast under trial" who will "receive the crown of life" (James 1:12).

The way to victory is through faith in Jesus the Son of God (2:18). That title embraces all that He is and all that He has done (1 John 5:4-5). That is a reminder of the way each letter began.

Kept by His Power

The "hour of trial" (3:10) probably refers to the same time of trouble referred to later in the book as "the great tribulation" (7:14). The use of a different Greek word in each case may be because the trouble is seen to have two different purposes.

The word for "trial" is mostly used for trouble that has a good purpose. During hard times people are more likely to turn to God than when things are going well. The "hour of trial" will give "the whole world" and "those who dwell on the earth" (3:10) an impetus and another opportunity to turn to Him.

On the other hand, trouble suffered by the Lord's people may be used by the evil one in an attempt to turn them away from Him. The work of God in our lives always has two parts to it, ours and His. For their part the Christians of Philadelphia have "kept [Christ's] word about patient endurance". Christ's part is to "keep them from the hour of trial". Later John is shown those who were "coming out of the great tribulation" (7:14). They had endured patiently and the Lord had kept them safe (1 Pet.1:3-5).

Right of Access

The Lord will make the victor a pillar in God's house (3:12). Pillars are a permanent part of the structure of a building. The promise is of a permanent place in God's presence and the victor will never go out of it. They will be given the name of God to show that they belong to God. The name "of the new Jerusalem" will prove the victor's rights as a citizen of God's city.

When the kingdom is won and Christ is exalted over all, His new name will be revealed (19:12). The whole of creation will see Him in His real character and, since they belong to Him, victors will bear that name. They will share in His glory (John 17:22).

The victor will be given a white stone with that new name written on it (2:17). A number of tentative suggestions have been put forward as to the significance of the stone. None of them is very convincing. But the inscribed stone referred to in one of the visions given to Zechariah may give some help in understanding the stone in Revelation.

In the vision the LORD said that He had given Joshua the high priest a stone (Zech.3:9). The inscription on it was probably God's promise to remove iniquity in a single day, a promise which was fulfilled at Calvary. Joshua and his fellow-priests and the rituals they performed were a symbol of that fulfilment. The idea was probably that Joshua had to carry that stone with him when he entered God's presence in the temple to perform his priestly duties. The promise on the stone gave validity to those symbolic sacrifices. Without that validity, entering God's presence would have proved fatal. Carrying the stone with the promise gave Joshua "right of access" (Zech.3:7) into God's presence.

The stone in Revelation could be intended to represent proof of identity. It bore the new name given to the victor and would guarantee the bearer right of access into God's presence. Paul wrote that we have this right of access through our Lord Jesus Christ (Rom.5:2).

Everlasting Life

In ancient cities a register was kept of those who lived there. When any citizen died their name was erased from the book. The names of the victors will never be erased (3:5) because they "will not be hurt by the second death" (2:11). The second death will be when "the dead, great and small" stand before God's throne (20:12). All that is evil and those whose names are not written in the register, "the book of life", will be "thrown into the lake of fire" (20:14-15).

For the victors, life will be everlasting. They will have access to the tree of life (2:7). When Adam and Eve disobeyed God they were banished from Eden lest they should eat of the tree of life and live forever in their sin (Gen.3:22-24). With sin finally dealt with, victors have access to the tree of life which grows by the river that flows from the throne of God (22:1-2, 14).

Christ "will give some of the hidden manna" to the one who conquers (2:17). When Jesus called upon people to believe in Him, they demanded a sign from Him to prove that He was worth following (John 6:30). Moses, they said, had proved his worth by giving their ancestors manna, "bread from heaven" (John 6:31). Jesus replied that God who had given the manna was also giving "the true bread from heaven" (John 6:32), "the food that endures to eternal life" (John 6:27). He went on to say that He is the bread of life and that whoever comes to Him shall not hunger, and whoever believes in Him shall never thirst (John 6:35).

Christ is the hidden manna. It is hidden because to benefit from the nourishment He gives requires faith: it is those who believe in Him who will neither hunger nor thirst.

Reigning with Christ

"The victor will sit with Christ on His throne" (3:21). Sitting on the throne was the highest honour. Since Christ is King of kings, to sit with Him on His throne is the highest honour possible. He conquered by being obedient to the point of death on a cross (Phil.2:8). He calls His followers to the same kind of obedience (Matt.16:24).

The Lord will give the one who conquers authority over the nations (2:26-27). The victor will be sitting with Christ on His throne so his authority will stem from Christ and be of the same kind. The King of kings subdues the nations by the sword which comes from His mouth (19:15), the armies of heaven following Him (19:14). The one who conquers exercises authority by what he says. He has the authority to proclaim to the world that Jesus is the Way and the Truth and the Life, and that no-one comes to the Father except through Him (John 14:6). The victor will rule "with a rod of iron". He will be unbending in maintaining that those who reject this one way to God will perish (20:15; 2 Cor.2:15-16).

With Christ Forever

Jesus Christ will give the victor "the morning star" (2:28). Christ is the morning star (22:16), so the promise is that He will give Himself to the one who conquers.

Morning stars are the last stars to appear in the east before sunrise. The Lord Jesus is not merely one of the morning stars but "the morning star", the last star to appear before the dawn breaks (2 Pet.1:19). When the dawn of eternity breaks all shadows will flee away and union with Christ will be complete (Song 2:17).

The one who conquers will be dressed in white (3:4-5). They will be clothed in Christ's righteousness with nothing of which to feel shame or to wish to hide. More than that, Jesus says, "They will walk with me." In heaven they will have the same righteous status as Christ.

The Lord promises that He will declare openly that the victor belongs to Him (3:5). The one who conquers will know that they belong in God's presence. They will always be with the Lord (1Thess.4:17).

3. Heaven's Perspective
Revelation 4:1 to 5:14
The Invitation

"After this I looked" indicates that the vision of the Risen Christ dictating His messages to the Church had faded and a new vision had begun. "And behold", wonder of wonders, there is a door open in heaven! This is not the sky (12:12), or the heavens of the sun, moon and stars (Psa.8:3), or the arena in which spiritual battles are fought (Eph.6:12). It is not those realms which are to be made new (21:1). A door is open into the place where God dwells and where He reveals Himself and heavenly realities.

John heard a voice speaking to him. It was like "the first voice" which he had heard, the one which sounded "like a trumpet", the voice of Jesus Christ risen from the dead (1:10).

The Lord invited John, "Come up here". The open door was not merely an opening through which the apostle might catch glimpses of heaven. John was invited to go right in so that he could see things clearly. "At once," John wrote, "I was in the Spirit." Immediately, not through any effort on John's part, but as a result of Christ's commanding voice, John was completely taken up with spiritual realities to the exclusion of earthly things.

The purpose of the invitation was that John could be shown things that would take place after his time. These things are recorded in chapters 6 to 22. But first John would be shown divine realities.

God Reigns

The first thing that caught John's eye was a throne and the One who sat upon it (4:2). This throne is mentioned forty times in Revelation, compared to only three times for Satan's throne which he gave to the beast (2:13; 13:2; 16:10). It is "the throne of God and of the Lamb" (22:1, 3). It is the throne of

God who loved the world by sending His only Son (John 3:16). It is the throne of the Lamb "who loves us and freed us from our sins by His blood" (1:5).

John was told that the events which he would be shown "must take place" (4:1). They must take place because they would be in accordance with the sovereign will of God. Many of the events would seem disastrous and the Church would, throughout them all, be a suffering Church. But the Church would know that all those things were issuing from the throne of love.

The One who sat on the throne "had the appearance of jasper and carnelian" (4:3). It is impossible to be absolutely certain what stones are meant. But jasper does occur as a deep crimson and carnelian is scarlet. The point of these fiery colours may be to stress God's attitude of judgment towards evil (20:14-15).

Around the throne John saw a rainbow. Perhaps the combination of judgment and a rainbow is a reminder of God's judgment on the world through the Flood and the rainbow which He gave afterwards as a reminder of His covenant never to flood the earth again (Gen.9:12-16).

The rainbow "had the appearance of an emerald" (4:3). Green is the colour of growth and hence of food and of life and hence of God's merciful and gracious provision. In contrast to the fiery colours of jasper and carnelian, the rainbow may represent mercy. While all that is evil and all those who persist in their antagonism towards God will experience His judgment, those who accept salvation through the Lamb will experience His mercy. The rainbow John saw was a ring around the throne: "mercy triumphs over judgment" (Jas.2:13). The ring was complete: the new covenant in Christ is eternal.

God Speaks

The lightning and thunder that issue from the throne are familiar metaphors in the poetry of the Old Testament. They are used to symbolise God's power especially when dealing with His enemies (1 Sam.2:10). They are also used to represent God speaking in power and majesty (Job 37:4). It seems that at Sinai the thunder and lightning conveyed both the idea of God's power which terrified the Israelites (Ex.19:16) and His voice when He spoke to Moses (Ex.19:9, 19).

That may also be the idea in John's vision. The word which NIV and ESV translate as "rumblings" can mean "voices" (KJV and RSV) especially when used in connection with people.

God speaks. His word comes with great power and achieves His purposes. This may be the connection in the vision between the lightning and thunder and the seven torches. The latter represent "the seven spirits of God" which are "sent out into all the earth" (5:6). The Spirit reminds His people of the teaching of Jesus (John 14:26), He guides "into all the truth" (John 16:13) and He "convicts the world concerning sin and righteousness and judgment" (John 16:8).

God Inaccessible

John recorded that "before the throne there was as it were a sea of glass, like crystal" (4:6).

Some have linked this with the "sea" that Solomon had made and erected in front of the entrance to the temple (1 Kings 7:23-26). But that account is all about the construction and dimensions of the bowl and its supports. Nothing is said about its contents except that it had a capacity of about 11,000 gallons.

John has nothing to say about a container. He writes about the "sea" itself. He does not say that he saw a sea but "as it were a sea". It was "like crystal", like clear glass. Most ancient glass was semi-opaque. Clear glass was enormously expensive and its magnificence was considered especially suitable for royalty. The "sea" is a symbol of God's majesty. It may also be a symbol of a shining ocean that forms an impassable barrier between sinful humans and a holy God.

God of Grace

Immediately after noticing the central throne and the One seated on it, John's attention is drawn to twenty-four other thrones on which are seated twenty-four elders (4:4).

In John's vision of the New Jerusalem, the gates are inscribed with the names of the twelve tribes of Israel (21:12) and the foundations bear the names of the twelve apostles (21:14). Since the New Jerusalem represents the Church, it is probable that the twenty-four elders represent the members of the Church. Each member of the Church has been given righteousness in Christ (Rom.3:24; Rom.5:17) and so are clothed in white (7:9).

The elders are seen sitting on thrones and wearing golden crowns. God in His mercy, love and grace has "raised us up with Christ and seated us with Him in the heavenly places in Christ Jesus" (Eph.2:4-6). Those who have received God's free gift of righteousness will "reign in life through the one man, Jesus Christ" (Rom.5:17). In eternity this will be completely fulfilled. They will be absolutely free from sin and will reign with Christ forever.

Through Christ a way has been made across the otherwise impassable crystal sea. He is "able to save to the uttermost those who draw near to God through Him" (Heb.7:25). Through Him both Jews and Gentiles "have access in one Spirit to the Father" (Eph.2:18).

God of Creation

On each side of the central throne John saw four living creatures (4:6-7). The "four winds of heaven" (Zech.2:6) and the "four corners of the earth" (Isa.11:12) are expressions which refer to the whole world. The four living creatures represent the whole of creation as the elders do the whole Church.

One creature was like a lion, the noblest of beasts; another was like an ox, the strongest; another had "the face of a man", the wisest; the fourth was "like an eagle in flight", the swiftest. These four, representing the best of all creation as God intended it to be, are in God's presence. It is God's purpose that creation will be set free from corruption and decay and will share in the glorious freedom that the children of God will enjoy (Rom.8:19-21).

There are many similarities between these creatures and those Ezekiel saw in his vision of the LORD God (Ezek.1:5-14). In that vision they were seen serving Him by forming a sort of chariot for His throne. Also, in John's vision, they were seen serving God in that they were "on each side of the throne". They were "full of eyes in front and behind", providing unlimited vigilance and awareness.

The living creatures were ceaselessly praising God by proclaiming that He is "Holy, holy, holy" (4:8). In Hebrew, repetition is used to express totality. For instance, in Genesis 14:10 where, in English, it says that a valley was "full of pits", the Hebrew is simply "pits, pits". Only in relation to the holiness of God is the word repeated three times (Isa.6:3).

God is absolutely holy. In His person He is completely opposite to anything seen in the world. He is the One "who was and is and is to come" (4:8). He is eternal. He is God "from everlasting to everlasting" (Psa.90:2).

The representatives of creation as they praise God seem to mean more than simply that He is eternal. God's holiness, His might and His eternal being are one subject of their praise. He is holy in that He is completely separate from creation. In

His might He created all things. In His eternal being He continues to sustain all things for His glory (Rom.11:36).

Whenever the living creatures praise God, the elders fall down and worship (4:9; 5:14). They take off their crowns and throw them down before the throne to show their submission to His authority and to acknowledge that they have crowns only by His mercy and grace.

It is curious that the elders apparently follow the lead of the living creatures. The Church led in praise and worship by creation? God's eternal power and divine nature are clearly revealed in what He has made (Rom.1:19-21). Perhaps that is the "lead" given by creation. The fact that the elders worship God because He created and sustains all things (4:11) would seem to support that.

The Scroll

John's eyes went back to the throne and the One seated on it. He saw, in God's hand, a scroll (5:1). The scroll was written on both sides of the papyrus leaving no space for additions or for editing. This was because it expressed God's sovereign will for the whole of creation.

It was, literally, "on" God's hand. It was not being grasped tightly but was lying there for anyone who was fit to approach the throne of the holy and almighty God, to pick it up. But a mighty angel, with a voice powerful enough to ensure that the whole universe could hear, proclaimed an awesome message. That was that whoever picked it up would not only have to be fit to approach God but must also be worthy to break the seals and open the scroll (5:2), thus executing God's sovereign will.

As the following chapters show, God's will includes the destruction of Satan and all his works and all who serve him. It follows that to be worthy, the one who took up the scroll had to be as just as God. It required someone who had conquered sin in his own life so as not to act from selfish ambition (Phil.2:3-5). He would do only what was just, right and good.

Although none could have failed to hear the angel's voice, at first no-one took up the challenge. This caused John to weep bitterly (5:4). He wept because unless God's sovereign will was carried out, the Church would continue to suffer, Satan would reign supreme, evil would prosper, all good would be overwhelmed and justice would never be done. The prospect was bleak indeed.

The Lamb

John was told to stop weeping because one had been found who was worthy to open the scroll (5:5). He was told that it is "the Lion of the tribe of Judah". When Jacob on his death-bed blessed his sons, he called Judah a lion (Gen.49:9-10). He said that Judah would hold the ruler's sceptre until the one came to whom the nations would be obedient.

The one who has been proved worthy is also described as "the Root of David". Isaiah foretold that although the Davidic monarchy would come to an end like a felled tree, when God sent His king he would be "a branch from [David's] roots" (Isa.11:1). Jesus was of the tribe of Judah and was descended from David. But He was more than a "son of David", He was David's Lord (Matt.22:42-45). He was born to be king (Matt.2:2), to rule "on the throne of David" forever (Isa.9:6-7).

But He died on a Roman cross and His title was fixed to the cross as an accusation and in mockery (John 19:19). John looked for this Lion King but what He saw was a Lamb, a Lamb "as though it had been slain" (5:6). Yet John was told that He had conquered.

The apostle Paul told how it came about. The Son of God left the glories of heaven and became a man. He was God's Servant and obeyed His Father to the point of death on a cross. Because of that total obedience, God has highly exalted him and given Him a name and status above all others. It is the Father's purpose that every knee will bow to Jesus Christ and own Him Lord (Phil.2:5-11). He has conquered through total obedience and is fit and able to execute the Father's will (cf. Matt.28:18).

It may be significant that it was one of the elders who told John the good news (5:5). Who better to tell him, and who could be more pleased? If Christ had not conquered there would be no Church and none to sit around the throne in white and wearing golden crowns.

John saw the Lamb "among the elders" (5:6). Is this an echo of Christ in the midst of the lampstands (1:13) but in a more personal way (cf. Matt.18:20)? Or is it a reminder that "one like a son of man" would be given "dominion and glory and a kingdom" (Dan.7:13-14)?

Or perhaps it is to emphasize the close relationship He has with His people. Other than in Revelation the word used for lamb occurs only in John 21:15. It means "little lamb" and is a term of endearment. Jesus called His disciples "friends" (John 15:15). He is not ashamed to call "brothers" those who have accepted His salvation (Heb.2:11). The Church is the Bride of the Lamb (21:9).

The Response

The living creatures and the twenty-four elders had been worshipping the One on the throne (4:8-10). But when the Lamb took the scroll they fell down before the Him (5:8). The blessings and honour ascribed to "our Lord and God" (4:11) were ascribed to the Lamb (5:12) and then to both together (5:13). John will see the Lamb "in the midst of the throne" (7:17), that is, at the centre of all power and authority. The throne is described as "the throne of God and of the Lamb" (22:1).

The Lamb shares the worship and the throne with the Father. The reason for that is that He was slain (5:9). By His death He has paid the ransom for people "from every tribe and language and people and nation" to set them free from Satan's tyranny.

The living creatures and the elders, representing as they evidently do those who have been set free, sing a new song. It is new because they are not merely repeating the words of some liturgy, but they are singing from their hearts in gratitude for all that the Lamb has achieved for them. The "golden bowls full of incense" being "the prayers of God's people" (NIV) seem to represent the whole Church falling down in praise, worship and gratitude.

God had rescued David from death and, in response, David sang a new song (Psa.144:9-10). He used a harp to help him in that, as the elders also did.

The praise and worship flowed out beyond the elders and living creatures to an uncountable number of angels (5:11-12) and beyond them to every living creature (5:13). The whole of creation, made new through the blood of the Lamb, was occupied in praising and worshipping Him.

The Backdrop

These chapters provide a view of heaven's perspective on history. This must be kept in mind as the Revelation continues. They set the scene for all that follows.

God speaks with power so that His word is always fulfilled. By His grace and through the Cross He has brought those whom He chose before the world began (Eph.1:4) to sit with Christ in the heavenly places, clothed in white, absolutely secure and safe from all evil. He made all things and continues to be in total control of His creation. This is the One who sits on the throne and rules with all authority and power.

Because the Lamb has conquered, all authority and power have been given to Him. He has the authority to break the seals. The events that are shown in the following visions happen only when He breaks each seal. Every event, however disastrous it may seem, is completely under His control.

Of course, there will be a fulfilment when the Church is complete, and when all creation is made new and worships Him. But these two chapters are not primarily about the way things will be but about the way things are. If this is lost sight of, the events themselves become more important than God's purpose in them. That will result in attempts to match vision with history and so lead to questions about when things will happen.

4. The Seals
Matthew 24 and Revelation 6:1 to 7:17
Jesus' Predictions

When Jesus' disciples began enthusing about the temple buildings, He warned them that the whole structure would be demolished. This seemed to them to be so drastic that it must herald "the end of the age" and, therefore, of His coming. In reply, Jesus described the kind of thing that would happen in the years leading up to His return.

All those things are matched in John's vision of the opening of the seals. The "wars and rumours of wars" (Matt.24:6) is matched by what follows the opening of the first seal. The troubles of Matthew 24:7 follow the opening of the second, third and fourth seals. The Lord's warning about persecution and death, and His encouragement to endure to the end (Matt.24:9-14) are reflected in the revealing of the souls of the martyrs when the fifth seal is opened.

The celestial disasters predicted by Jesus (Matt.24:29) take place after the opening of the sixth seal. This is soon to be followed by the coming of "the Son of Man" (Matt.24:30), and the day of the wrath of God and of the Lamb (Rev.6:15-17).

Some things Jesus said are not matched in Revelation. The prophecy about the fall of Jerusalem (Matt.24:15-28) was fulfilled in AD70 and so had already happened when John was shown the visions. The Lord's warnings not to be led astray by false christs or jump to conclusions about timing (24:4-5, 6, 8, 23-28) are not repeated in Revelation, but need to be observed as events unfold in real life. Jesus' prediction that "this generation" would not pass away until "all these things take place" (Matt.24:34) is usually taken to refer to the destruction of Jerusalem and the other indications that Christ's return is imminent.

The First Seal
The Lamb opened the first seal and one of the four living creatures gave the command, "Come out!" (6:1 CEV). What "came out" (6:2) was a rider on a white horse.

Later John again saw a rider on a white horse (19:11-21). Those who would identify the rider in 6:2 with that one, say that the phrase "and to conquer" signifies permanent victory. This is held to refer to Christ's final victory over all evil (19:19-21).

But the rider of chapter 19 is clearly identified as "the Word of God" and as "King of kings and Lord of lords". He is followed by the armies of heaven and wages war on all evil with the sword which comes from His mouth.

The rider in 6:2 is alone and is given a bow. He is the first in a series of riders who are called out to wreak death and destruction on earth. The NIV renders the words "and to conquer" as, "he rode out as a conqueror bent on conquest", and GNB and CEV give the words a similar meaning.

In Jesus' equivalent prediction, He told His disciples not to be alarmed. That would not be appropriate if He was speaking of His victory and the victorious spread of the Gospel. His coming would not be until after times of war, famine, earthquake and great tribulation.

The opening of the first seal gave the evil one the power (a bow) and the authority (a crown) to conquer. This he would achieve by luring world rulers into an attempt to achieve world domination by worshipping him (cf. Matt.4:8-9). Perhaps the horse being white relates to the fact that "Satan disguises himself as an angel of light" (2 Cor.11:14). He would "give his throne" to rulers (cf. 13:2) and so rule the world through them. The result would be "wars and rumours of wars".

The Second Seal
The second horse was red. This may refer to the

bloodshed which would result from its coming. The rider was given permission to remove peace from the earth so that people would kill one another.

The outcome of the opening of the first seal was the kind of war which is waged as one nation seeks to conquer another. The rider on the red horse brings something different. Although he is given a great sword, it is the people who would do the killing. It would mean world wars in which millions would die, often without really knowing what they were fighting for. It would mean civil wars and murder. Killing would become an everyday occurrence. It would lead to the knife crimes which are increasingly common in our country.

The rider is "permitted" to exert this influence in the world. It is as Jesus said of the wars the disciples would hear of, "This must take place." (Matt.24:6). The riders are summoned out by the commands of the living creatures. All these things happen according to God's sovereign authority. As often seen in the Old Testament, God uses human history to carry out His purposes of salvation and judgment.

The Third Seal

The opening of the third seal introduces a time when, perhaps as a result of war, food is scarce. The rider had a pair of scales in his hand. Food is to be weighed out, rationed.

A quart of wheat was enough food for one man for one day. A denarius was one day's wages. A single man could live from hand to mouth, he could get by.

He would be able to buy three quarts of barley a day. He would have to do this if he had dependants. But barley is less nourishing than wheat, so that, in time, the family would become malnourished.

Why the oil and wine are protected is not clear. Perhaps God in His mercy made this decree to give some comfort in those difficult times. Times would be hard and people would suffer, but God would set the limits both on the scarcity of the food and on the availability of things that bring comfort.

The Fourth Seal

At the opening of the fourth seal things go from bad to worse. People do not merely suffer hunger and malnutrition, but death.

The first three riders carried emblems of the authority they had been given, a bow and a crown (6:2), a great sword (6:4) or a pair of scales (6:5). The rider of the pale horse carries no emblem but he has a name and a companion. His name is Death and his companion is Hades.

Hades is the realm of the dead. In the Old Testament it is called in Hebrew "Sheol". It is a place of darkness (Job 10:21), forgetfulness (Psa.88:12), silence (Psa.94:17) and total weakness (Psa.88:4). In the realm of the dead are those whom God has forgotten and who are cut off from Him (Psa.88:5). It is a place from which there was no hope of escape until Christ came (1:18).

Death's aim is to bring everyone down to Hades and keep them there. He would use "sword, famine, pestilence and wild beasts" (6:8), which God describes as His "four disastrous acts of judgment" (Ezek.14:21).

Death is given authority to do that for a quarter of the earth's population. Whether or not that was to happen all in one place or distributed throughout the earth, all at once or spread over the centuries, we are not told. But the four methods of killing, one in four being killed and this being the fourth seal probably convey the idea that the whole world will feel the effects (cf. "the four corners of the earth" in Isa.11:12).

The Fifth Seal

When the fifth seal was opened there was no command "Come!", and no horse and rider appeared. Instead John saw, "under the altar" the souls of those who had been killed for faithfully telling God's message of salvation through His Son Jesus.

There has been some discussion as to which altar this was. That is probably no more to the point than the question of how Hades was following Death (6:8), on the same horse or on his own. The significance of the altar is that these people had given their lives sacrificially in the service of their Lord and Master (cf. Rom.12:1-2; Phil.2:17; 2 Tim.4:6).

Their souls cried out for vengeance "on those who dwell on earth". In Revelation this phrase refers, not to the whole human race, but to those who remain opposed to God, His works and His people (3:10; 8:13; cf. 6:15).

They are told to rest a little longer – more martyrs would be joining them. They had come to Christ and found rest for their souls (Matt.11:28). They had served Him faithfully to death. They could continue to rest in the knowledge that their Lord is Sovereign and would carry through His purposes. He is "holy and true", a God of justice (Deut.32:4).

Meanwhile they were each given a white robe. Perhaps this was to serve as a reminder of God's gift of righteousness (Rom.5:17) and of the security of their future – they would walk with Christ in white (3:4; 7:13-14).

The Sixth Seal

At the opening of the sixth seal there was a great earthquake. Earthquakes occur again after the opening of the seventh seal (8:1-5), at the end of the events following the blowing of the sixth trumpet (9:13 - 11:13), and at the pouring out of the seventh bowl (16:17-18).

Just as real earthquakes will test buildings so that those which have not been built to withstand them will collapse, so the earthquakes of these visions symbolise the testing and inevitable destruction of all that is opposed to God (16:19-21; Heb.12:27-28). The whole present order will come to an end

(6:12-14) and God will make all things new (21:1, 5).

The collapse of the existing system will usher in the great day of the wrath of God and of the Lamb. It will introduce the return of the Lord as Judge (Acts 17:31), and those who have persisted in their rejection of Him will be terrified (6:15-17).

Four Winds

After the opening of six of the seals, John is shown four angels holding back "the four winds of the earth". They were preventing any gale-force wind from causing damage to the earth, the sea or the trees (7:1-2).

In the Old Testament, winds are used as symbols of the outpouring of God's judgment. When God pronounced judgment on Elam, He spoke of bringing upon that land "the four winds from the four quarters of heaven" (Jer.49:36). So the angels seen by John were delaying the onset of God's judgment and were instructed to do so until the servants of God had been sealed (7:3).

The Old Testament prophet Zechariah was shown, in a vision, four horses, or four groups of horses, which had been patrolling the earth for God (Zech.1:8-10). After reporting to God, they were then sent out in judgment pulling chariots (Zech.6:1-8). When the prophet asked what they were, the answer given was literally, "These are the four winds of heaven" (Zech.6:5).

The four horsemen of Zechariah are matched by "the four horsemen of the apocalypse" which come out as the first four seals are opened to execute God's judgment upon the earth. The four winds are another way of representing the four horsemen. Their work was to be delayed until the sealing was complete.

144,000

It is not easy to be absolutely certain who those sealed are. The first thing to notice is that they are "the servants of our God" (7:3). The word for servants is literally "slaves" and denotes total devotion to God. These are those who have "endured to the end". So it was fitting that they should be sealed with "the seal of the living God", the mark of God's ownership. This would not mean they would be protected from all suffering (6:9) but that their eternal future was secure.

This is not the first time in Revelation that specific instructions were given about named groups of people. John was told to write for the seven named churches, not only the letters addressed to them but what he would see (1:11). If that is to be taken literally then this book has nothing to do with me and I can stop trying to understand it. But, as was seen, the seven churches are symbolic of the whole Church, and the book is a message for the Church for all time.

Similarly, 144,000 is a symbolic number. 12 is the number of Israel and 10 is a number of completeness. 144,000 = 12 x 12 x 10 x 10 x 10. As a symbol the number would mean the whole of Israel.

Israel and the Church

What is meant by Israel? The list of tribes given here presents problems. Dan is omitted. Joseph is included which, as a "tribe" would include the descendants of both his sons. But Manasseh is included, while his other son, Ephraim is not.

There are many instances in the New Testament of Christians, whether Jews or Gentiles, being referred to in terms which normally applied specifically to Jews. When Peter wrote to the Christians of what we know as northern Turkey, he called them "elect" or chosen (1 Pet.1:1; 1 Pet.2:9; cf. Deut.14:2). He told them, "Once you were not a people, but now you are God's people" (1 Pet.2:10). This was originally a promise made to the Jews of the northern kingdom of Israel (Hos.1:10; Hos.2:23).

Paul instructed Titus to teach the Christians of Crete that

God's purpose for them was to be "a people for his own possession" (Tit.2:14-15; cf. Deut.7:6). He told the Galatian Christians that since they were Christ's they were "Abraham's offspring" (Gal.3:29). Jews were known as "the circumcision" (Eph.2:11), but Paul wrote, "We are the circumcision, who worship by the Spirit of God and glory in Christ Jesus" (Phil.3:3).

God showed in the Old Testament that He always intended that His Church would include both Jews and Gentiles (Isa.2:2; Isa.49:6). It is clear in Paul's letters that the Church consists of both Jews and Gentiles without distinction (Gal.3:28). In the letter to the Romans it is sometimes difficult to know when he writes of "Israel" whether he is referring to the nation or to the Church. But he does make it clear that he saw the Church, not as a replacement for Israel but a continuation and fulfilment of it (Rom.11:17-18).

In trying to understand these verses it is worth bearing in mind that all Christians are sealed (2 Cor.1:22; 2 Cor.5:5; Eph.1:13-14). The Holy Spirit is the guarantee (KJV "earnest") that our eternal future is secure.

Yes I to the end shall endure
As sure as the earnest is given
More happy but not more secure
The glorified spirits in heaven
From "A debtor to mercy alone"
Augustus Montague Toplady (1740-1778)

The Great Multitude

John saw "a great multitude that no-one could number, from every nation, from all tribes and peoples and languages" (7:9). The list is comprehensive; it does not allow for any exceptions. It must include Jews as well as Gentiles.

The elder told John, "These are the ones coming out of the great tribulation" (7:14). Some think that this refers to martyrs. Some think that the "great tribulation" is the tribulation which will come at the end of all things (3:10).

If only martyrs were being referred to, the number would seem rather large, and other references to the martyrs are quite clear. For instance, martyrs are "those who had been slain for the word of God" (6:9). They are "those who had been beheaded for the testimony of Jesus" (20:4).

As for tribulation, Jesus said that it is what every believer must expect to experience (John 16:33).

If the explanation given by the elder had been particular and exclusive there would have been no need to say that those in the multitude had "washed their robes and made them white in the blood of the Lamb" (7:14). This is what every believer has done (1 Cor.6:11; Heb.9:14).

John **heard** "the number of the sealed" (7:4), but what he **saw** was "a great multitude that no-one could number" (7:9). Perhaps this means that, from heaven's point of view, the number sealed is complete and God knows each one (2 Tim.2:19). They are God's Israel, His chosen people. But from an earthly point of view it is a countless multitude from every nation on earth.

Service and Security

The multitude serve God as King (7:15). As priests to the God and Father of Jesus Christ (1:6), they serve Him continuously in His temple. This temple is not some building within heaven (21:22) but heaven itself, the very presence of God, His sanctuary.

Their service is to acknowledge that they owe their salvation entirely to God and the Lamb (7:10). They carry palm branches which, together with the white robes signify victory through Christ (Rom.8:37; 1 Cor.15:57). The angels cry their agreement with "Amen!", which they repeat (7:12), and join in the praise and worship of God. What they say is literally "*the* blessing and *the* glory and *the* wisdom and *the* thanksgiving and *the* honour and *the* power and *the* might be to our God forever and ever". His glory is superior to all and not to be shared with another (Isa.42:8).

The redeemed will be sheltered by God's presence (7:15). The psalmist said that whoever goes to the Lord for safety can be confident of complete protection (Psa.91:1). As a bird covers her chicks with her wings to hide and protect them from predators, so the Lord protects those who trust in Him. His faithfulness is as sure as a shield or a city wall (Psa.91:4). They will not suffer in any conceivable way (7:16)

The Lamb will be their shepherd (7:17). What a remarkable reversal of roles! Can a lamb provide the care of a shepherd? But He is the Lamb that was slain for them so they can trust Him completely and follow where He leads. He will "guide them to springs of living water", to never-failing sources of on-going satisfaction (cf. John 4:10).

Each member of this great multitude will receive personal attention. God will wipe away every single tear. This comes from a Father who really cares (Matt.10:29-31).

The Seventh Seal

God's judgments have been carried out (6:1-8), the system of the universe has collapsed (6:12-14) and Christ has returned as Judge (6:15-17). Through those judgments believers have suffered (6:9-11) but they have been sealed with the seal of the living God and have been kept secure. John has been shown the Church enjoying the protection and blessings of God and the Lamb in the life to come.

What more is there to be shown? It might be expected that the opening of the seventh seal would introduce the things recorded in the last few chapters of this book. But, after a brief interlude (8:1), its opening introduces another round of seven plagues, each plague initiated by the blowing of a trumpet.

5. Trumpets and Bowls

Trumpets – Revelation 8:1 to 9:21; 11:15-19
Bowls – Revelation 15:1 to 16:21

A Spiral Staircase

It may help to compare moving through the chapters of Revelation to climbing a spiral staircase. In each full turn there are seven windows through which are to be seen visions of what God is doing. Through every first window we are shown the same scene but from a different perspective and with different details. The same applies to every second window, every third window, and so on.

At intervals John had, as it were, to step off the staircase into side-rooms (e.g. 10:1-11; 12:1-17) where he was shown other visions. These show in greater detail than the descriptions of the plagues what the enemy is trying to do and how God is frustrating the enemy's purpose and defeating him.

Eventually John reached the top of the staircase. The plagues introduced by the pouring out of the bowls "are the last, for with them the wrath of God is finished" (15:1). But there would be more visions to explain in yet more detail what God has planned both for His enemies and for those who are sealed with His seal.

The Silence

When the Lamb opened the seventh seal, the worship of the multitude and the angels (7:9-12) was silenced (8:1). This may have been because of the seriousness of what was about to happen when seven trumpets were blown.

Habakkuk foretold that God would bring the Chaldeans upon the Jews for their lawlessness and injustice during the reign of Jehoiakim (Hab.1:2-4; Jer.22:13-17). He said that the Chaldeans would be punished in their turn for plundering other nations (Hab.2:8) and for their excessive violence (Hab.2:17). Having pronounced these judgments the prophet said, "The LORD is in his holy temple; let all the earth keep silence before him." (Hab.2:20).

The Prayers

The silence may have been so that the prayers of God's people could be heard. John had been shown the souls of the martyrs crying out for vindication and justice (6:9-11). During this silence John saw "the prayers of all the saints" being offered with "much incense" (8:3). The saints are, of course, Christians (cf. Rom.16:15), not just those who have been "canonized".

The importance of these prayers is emphasised in several ways. Both the censer and the altar were golden. The angel was given the incense. The implication is that he received it directly or indirectly from God. The fact that the angel was given a substantial quantity of incense shows how highly God valued the prayers as does the fact that the prayers "rose before God" (8:4).

It is probably significant that the censer that was used to burn the incense to offer with the prayers was then used to throw fire from the altar on the earth (8:5). This resulted in a prelude to the blowing of the trumpets. It seems to show that the judgments that came at the blowing of the trumpets were in some way in response to those prayers. The seven angels were given the trumpets but they did not blow them until the prayers had risen before God.

It has been said that prayer moves the Hand that moves the world. The prayers of God's people are effective (Jas.5:16).

The Angels

John saw "the seven angels who stand before God" (8:2). In the Book of Tobit, a Jewish work probably written in the early second century BC, the angel Raphael says, "I am ... one of the seven who stand before the Lord" (Tobit 12:15). In another ancient Jewish book is written, "These are the angels who watch." This is followed by seven names including Michael and Gabriel (1 Enoch 20:1-7). As in all John's attempts to describe the visions he saw, he was using terms with which he was familiar.

The other angel (8:3) is not identified. He was not interceding for the saints. He was offering the incense to accompany the prayers which came from God's people. Jesus the Son of God intercedes for us (Heb.7:25) as does the Holy Spirit (Rom.8:27). The smoke from the incense rising with the prayers was a visual guarantee to John and his readers that the prayers were accepted.

The Warnings

Trumpets were used to give a warning (cf. Ezek.33:3). In John's vision, the purpose of each trumpet was to sound a warning rather than to launch complete destruction. This is shown by the fact that with the blowing of the first four trumpets the damage was limited to one third.

After the first trumpet a third of the earth and plants were burnt. After the second a third of the sea was turned to blood, a third of sea creatures died and a third of ships were destroyed. It was one third of rivers and springs that were polluted by Wormwood after the third trumpet was blown. When the fourth trumpet was blown, the balance between light and darkness, day and night was upset (8:12).

It could be seen that the severity of the warnings increased. People could survive on two thirds of plants and fresh water, and those who did not go to sea were not immediately affected by the damage there. But then everyone would be affected by the upset in the balance of day and night.

Things would get worse, and a warning was given to that effect by an eagle (8:13). But the damage that followed the blowing of the fifth and sixth trumpets continued to be limited. The torment of the scorpion stings would last for five months

(9:5) not for a complete year. The four angels at the Euphrates were released to kill only one third of mankind (9:15).

The Star

Many suggestions have been made as to the identity of the star (9:1). It was evidently intended to be understood as personal since it was given a key with which it opened the shaft of the bottomless pit (9:2). If the star represents Christ Himself this part of the vision could be meant to show men suffering the results of their rejection of Him and His Gospel.

The one who rules in the bottomless pit is called Abaddon, which is Hebrew for "destruction", or Apollyon, which is a Greek word meaning "Destroyer" (9:11). This clearly means Satan (cf. 20:1-3). The bottomless pit is not the place of the dead but is inhabited by the spiritual forces which are opposed to God.

When people reject Christ and His Gospel, they open their hearts and lives to the forces of evil. This may be what this vision is intended to show. It certainly fits in with the rest of what happened when the fifth trumpet was blown.

The Locusts

When describing an invasion of locusts an Old Testament prophet wrote, "Their appearance is like the appearance of horses, and like war horses they run." (Joel 2:4). In his vision John saw locusts rising in the smoke from the bottomless pit. "In appearance the locusts were like horses prepared for battle" (9:7). Locusts' heads are shaped rather like those of horses. They move together in ranks like lines of mounted soldiers. The noise of their wings was like military horses charging (9:9). So, as with the prophet, it is their appearance rather than their size that is the point here.

But John is describing creatures which are far from natural. The best he can do by way of description is to say that "on their heads were **what looked like** crowns of gold", and so on (9:7-10). Like scorpions, they have stings in their tails and that is where their power to hurt lies (9:10). Natural locusts have no leaders (cf. Prov.30:27), but these locusts are led by Abaddon/Apollyon who is Satan. These locusts represent the demons which people persist in worshipping (9:20).

The Four Angels

The voice from the four horns of the altar (9:13) may be another allusion to God answering the prayers of saints. Or the voice may be that of the angel who was given the incense.

The Euphrates formed the eastern limit of the Promised Land (Gen.15:18; Josh.1:4). The angels being bound outside the Promised Land may be another symbol of God's protection of His people and His work; the power of the evil one is limited. The angels were released at the exact hour (9:15) that God had determined. God is in complete control.

When the angels were released, John's attention was immediately drawn to mounted troops. The four angels must have been the leaders of the troops. John "*heard* their number" (9:16). This symbolises the fact that the troops were too numerous to count.

The colours of the breastplates matched what came from the horses' mouths, and that is what killed (9:18). Their tails were "like serpents with heads", and they inflicted wounds by them (9:19; cf. 9:10).

Repentance

When Revelation is read it is often the disasters themselves that catch and keep the reader's attention. What is often missed is the fact that God instigates all of the plagues and remains in complete control. The seven angels were **given** the trumpets, and they had to wait until God had heard His people's prayers. The star was **given** a key (9:1). The locusts were **given** power (9:3) and were **allowed** to torment people (9:5) but not to kill. Those who had the seal of God on their foreheads were protected from harm (9:4). The command to release the four angels came from the altar (9:13-14).

God had a purpose in the blowing of the trumpets and that was that people should heed the warnings and repent. They are presented as being guilty of worshipping demons (cf. 1 Cor.10:20) and dumb idols, and of murder, sorcery, sexual immorality and theft (9:20-21). The sad end to these six warnings is that those who were not killed by the plagues ignored them and did not repent.

The Seventh Trumpet

When the seventh trumpet was blown a proclamation was made that "The kingdom of the world has become the kingdom of our Lord and of his Christ, and he shall reign forever and ever." (11:15). John was to be shown a number of visions which were to demonstrate how the reign of Christ would be put into effect.

Before that, the details of chapter 15 were given to form a prelude to the main event. This is the pouring out of the bowls and the resulting plagues. The chapter provides a backdrop against which the plagues may be seen and understood.

God's Deeds

These plagues are "great and amazing" (15:1) because they are God's deeds (15:3). He is the Lord God the Almighty, having greater power than any other (Isa.40:17-25). He is "King of the nations" and they can no more resist Him than can dust (Isa.40:15).

The fact that these plagues are God's doing is emphasised several times in these chapters. The seven angels came "out of the sanctuary" (15:6), that is, from the presence of God. The command to pour out the bowls came from the same place (16:1). Since the sanctuary had been closed to all (15:8), the "loud voice" must have been the voice of God. The plagues were recognised as God's judgments (16:5, 7). It was "God who had power over these plagues" (16:9; cf. 16:21). The last battle will be "on the great day of God the Almighty" (16:14). It was God who "remembered Babylon the great" to ensure that her punishment was meted out to her in full (16:19).

Babylon represents the operational centre of mankind organised in opposition to God. For the churches to which this was written it would have been understood to mean Rome.

It is as if, in this vision of the final outpouring of His wrath against evil (15:1), God Himself was understood to be taking direct action.

No Limits

"The sanctuary of the tent of witness" (15:5) refers back to the "tent of meeting" of the Old Testament. Into that tent God accepted the approaches of the High Priest when he entered to make atonement for Israel (Lev.16). But, for the duration of the plagues, entrance to the tent was blocked. The opportunity for pleading with God for mercy and accepting His grace was over. The plagues would proceed unchecked.

The only limitation set on the plagues was that the sores of the first plague were suffered by those who gave total allegiance to the beast (16:2). Once again, those bearing God's seal are shown to be protected.

Otherwise, in contrast to the thirds affected by the trumpet plagues, the devastation resulting from the pouring out of the bowls was total. All sea was turned to blood and everything in it died (16:3; ct. 8:8-9). All rivers and springs became blood (16:4; ct. 8:10-11). The effect on the sun was total (16:8-9; ct. 8:12).

The Bowls

The first mention of golden bowls is of those held by the four living creatures and the twenty-four elders as they worshipped around the throne (5:8). Those bowls full of incense are said to be "the prayers of the saints". The golden bowls given by one of the living creatures to the angels (15:7) may be another reminder of the effectiveness of the prayers of God's people.

In the Old Testament God used the image of a cup filled with intoxicating drink and drugs to illustrate how He would deal with those who defied Him (Isa.51:17, 22-23; cf. Ezek.23:32-34). He said that He would put such a cup into their hands so that they would drink it and become helpless. It was a cup of staggering. It was the cup of His wrath. The thought may be that a cupful is drunk relatively slowly and by choice. The offender could choose to put it down and turn back to God in repentance.

However, the golden bowls "full of the wrath of God" (15:7) were poured out on the earth (16:1). The contents gushed out upon the earth. There was no choice, there was no hope of escape. This was final (15:1).

But this was just. God's ways are "just and true" (15:3; 16:5). The altar, maybe representing the souls of the martyrs (6:9), agreed with that (16:7). Those suffering from these plagues were guilty of persecuting and killing God's servants and their sins have returned upon them. This is "what they deserve" (16:6).

The Enemies

The enemies of God are the dragon, the beast and the false prophet (16:13). The dragon is Satan (12:9), while the beast is the secular leader and the false prophet is the religious leader of mankind organised in opposition to God. The churches to which this was written would have understood the beast to be the Roman emperor.

People become enemies of God (Rom.5:6-10) by refusing to live in obedience to Him and, often unwittingly, living in obedience to the evil one. Just as God's people are sealed with

His seal (7:3; Eph.1:13), so those who serve the evil one bear "the mark of the beast" (16:2).

Christ fights by what He says (1:16; 19:15), and so do the dragon, the beast and the false prophet. In their case their words appeared to John like frogs coming out of their mouths (16:13). These frogs are really unclean, demonic spirits, which go out into the world to motivate world leaders to join forces in their fight against God (16:14).

God's Purpose

The Greek word translated "finished" (15:1) carries with it the idea of a purpose being achieved. What was achieved by these six plagues was not repentance. Those who suffered from the plagues only cursed God (16:9, 11, 21). God's purpose is that all evil shall be destroyed. In the pouring out of the fifth, sixth and seventh bowls that purpose is seen being achieved.

The fifth bowl was emptied onto the beast's throne and its kingdom was plunged into darkness (16:10). Walking in darkness will ultimately end in disaster. Perhaps the fifth bowl was intended as a final warning. This may be the reason why John says that the people of the beast's kingdom "did not repent of their deeds" (16:11).

By the outpouring of the sixth bowl, God's restraint on His enemies was removed and the way was made clear for them to unleash their forces (16:12-16). John was shown them assembling their armies at Armageddon.

There may be a reference in that name to the battle of Megiddo in Judges 4. Faced with a Canaanite army which had 900 iron chariots, Israel was outnumbered and "outgunned". But "the LORD routed Sisera and all his chariots and all his army before Barak by the edge of the sword" (Judg.4:15). Those gathering at Armageddon would have been deceived (19:20; 20:9-10) into thinking that victory was certain. But opposition to God always ends in disaster.

This is what happened when the seventh bowl was poured out into the air (16:17), the abode of demons (Eph.2:2). Babylon, the centre of operations of the beast, was split into three parts (16:19). A city divided against itself cannot stand (Mark 3:24). This judgment is seen as final and complete: God will make Babylon "***drain*** the cup of the wine of the fury of His wrath" (16:19). The cities of the kings who had been called to battle also fell.

God's purpose is that all evil shall be destroyed. Later visions make it clear that this purpose will be achieved (e.g. 19:11-21).

Historical Connections

Thinking about the three series of plagues in close succession may help to show the difficulties involved in interpreting them in terms of consecutive events in world history.

The universe was seen collapsing when the Lamb opened the sixth seal (6:12-14). But, when the fourth trumpet is blown, the universe is again in place. At the sound of that trumpet (8:12) one third of the sun and one third of the moon and one third of the stars were darkened. Then, at the outpouring of the fourth bowl (16:8), the sun is back to more than its full strength.

The opening of the sixth seal heralds the return of Christ as Judge (6:15-17). Opening the seventh seal introduces the series of the trumpet plagues. When the seventh trumpet sounds, the proclamation is made, "The kingdom of the world has become the kingdom of our Lord and of his Christ, and he shall reign forever and ever." (11:15). But it is not until the seventh bowl is poured out that there is an indication that victory in the battle against evil is imminent.

The plague following the blowing of the sixth trumpet (9:13-17) corresponds to the one following the pouring out of the sixth bowl (16:12-16). Both have to do with the release of armies of the enemy from the Euphrates, that is, from the east.

An angel announced that there would be no more delay, but that in the days of the seventh trumpet call, the mystery of God would be fulfilled (10:5-7). In view of that we might expect that, when all the trumpets have been blown, everything will have been accomplished. But John was taken further "up the spiral staircase". Yet another round of seven plagues begins with the pouring out of the bowls (15:1; 16:2). And it was revealed to John that the plagues of the bowls would be the last because "with them the wrath of God is finished" (15:1).

6. Faithfulness and Vindication

Revelation 10:1 to 11:14

The Angel

John saw an angel who had God's full authority. He came down from heaven, from God's presence, sent by God (10:1). He came wrapped in a cloud: the psalmist wrote that God "makes the clouds his chariot" (Psa.104:3). Over his head he had a rainbow: John had been shown God's throne encircled by a rainbow (4:3). His legs were "like pillars of fire": John would have been reminded that God had led the Israelites at night by a pillar of fire (Ex.13:21-22).

The angel swore an oath "by Him who lives for ever and ever" and who created everything (10:6). What the angel would proclaim would certainly come about because it was the God by whom he had sworn who would do it. The people of the earth would do well to listen to what the angel had to say.

The Message

In spite of the plagues which followed the blowing of the sixth trumpet, the people of earth did not repent (9:20-21). "Then", that is to say, immediately after being shown this, John saw the mighty angel descending from heaven (10:1). He had come with the message that the opportunity to repent was coming to an end. The blowing of the seventh trumpet (10:7) would prompt the pouring out of "the seven bowls of the wrath of God" (16:1) which would result in deadly and unavoidable plagues. This would be final (15:1). With these plagues God's plan for dealing with evil and saving His people would be complete: "the mystery of God would be fulfilled" (10:7).

The Mystery

The mystery of God is His plan of judgment and salvation which "He announced to His servants the prophets" (10:7). Throughout the Old Testament this plan had been gradually unfolded but not made completely clear until the Son of God came and lived and died and rose again. That mystery is "the mystery of the gospel" (Eph.6:19). It is "Christ in you, the hope of glory" (Col.1:27). It is Christ Himself (Col.2:2).

It has been the task of people like the apostle Paul to "bring to light for everyone what is the plan of the mystery hidden for ages in God" (Eph.3:9). The angel holds a scroll which is open for anyone to read.

The Thunders

In the vision, "the seven thunders sounded" when the angel called out (10:3). David wrote, "The voice of the LORD is over the waters; the God of glory thunders" (Psa.29:3). He went on to write six more times in that psalm of "the voice of the LORD", speaking of the great power of His voice (Psa.29:3, 4, 5, 7, 8, 9).

There was speech in the sound of the thunders (10:4) which John was about to write down. It is as if, at this crucial point in God's dealings with the world, God Himself is speaking.

Universal

The message was given in such a way that no-one would be able to say that they had not noticed or heard. As already noted, the scroll was open in his hand. The messenger was a "mighty angel" (10:1). He was so colossal that he was able to "set his right foot on the sea, and his left foot on the land" (10:2). His voice was so loud it was like a lion roaring (10:3). This was a voice intended to be audible to the whole world.

Partial

Not every detail is revealed in the visions of Revelation. The scroll which the Lamb took required seven seals, and only the Lamb could open it. In contrast, the one in the angel's hand was "a little scroll" (10:2). John was forbidden from writing down what was said through the seven thunders (cf. 2 Cor.12:3-4). This book does not give enough information to work out a detailed course of events for the last days. Its purpose is to enable an appropriate response to what happens in this world, in the light of what John wrote.

Final Warnings

At different times and in different places God has given final warnings. He is patient (2 Pet.3:9), continuing to discipline and warn, and to give time for repentance. When that is ignored
He has given notice that severe punishment will follow.

Pharaoh suffered nine plagues. After some he repented (Ex.8:8, 28; 9:27; 10:16-17), but then changed his mind and refused to let God's people go. The time came when there would be no further chance to repent (10:29), and the first-born of the Egyptians died.

God had warned the people of Israel of their sin through Elijah and Elisha. About one hundred years later the prophet Amos warned them that God would "not revoke the punishment" for their unjust treatment of the poor and for their immorality (Amos 2:6-7; cf. Hos.10:4-8). About forty years after Amos the people were deported and scattered throughout the Assyrian empire. The people of Judah followed a similar path and were exiled to Babylon.

The risen Lord sent a warning through John to the church in Ephesus (2:5). It seems that the warning was not heeded. There is no church in Ephesus today.

God's final call may also come to an individual:

Someday you'll hear God's Final Call to you
To take his offer of salvation true-
This could be it my friend if you but knew-
God's Final Call, God's Final Call.

© 1961 John W. Peterson Music Company. All rights reserved. Used by permission.

The day will come in which God's final call to the whole world will sound. After that, God will bring His mystery, His plan of salvation to a conclusion.

John's Task

The "voice from heaven" (cf. 10:4) spoke to John again and commanded him to take the scroll from the angel's hand. This may have been the voice of God. It was certainly authoritative for John since he obeyed it each time.

That it is the same angel is made clear by the description of his stance (10:2, 4, 8). It is the same open scroll, and the message is the same. The angel speaking in a loud voice to all the world is a vision. John has to actually deliver that message (10:11). Irenaeus and Jerome both claimed that John died in Ephesus. Perhaps he was released from Patmos and continued his preaching there. Or perhaps his prophesying again (10:11) refers to writing the rest of Revelation, and to its being read by so many down through the centuries.

The angel told John that he was to eat the scroll (10:9). He was told, literally, to "eat it down". That is to say, he was to make the message of the scroll part of him. It was to determine his way of thinking and what he would preach.

John was told that, initially, the scroll would taste sweet. No doubt the message that God would soon finish His plan, destroy His enemies and rescue His suffering Church was good to hear. To those who accept God's word and submit to it, it is sweet (Jer.15:15-16).

But as the message was absorbed the bitter aspects of it would become apparent. It is a joy to tell sinners that through Jesus there is forgiveness and restoration to fellowship with a heavenly Father. But, to those who really care, it is hard to tell of hell fire to those who reject the Gospel.

John had been told to take the scroll. He asked the angel to give it to him but was again told to take it. God calls us into

His service but our response is voluntary (cf. Isa.6:8). When we volunteer, He sends and empowers us.

A Secure Church

John was given a rigid measuring rod and told to measure the temple of God (11:1). In view of the fact that the temple in Jerusalem had been destroyed in AD 70 along with the city, this must be symbolic. Bearing in mind the flow of the chapter, it makes sense to take the rest of it as symbolic too.

Referring to the Church as God's temple would have been familiar to the early Church (1 Cor.3:16; 2 Cor.6:16; Eph.2:21-22). The altar may point to the grounds for access into God's presence. In the context (11:7-10) it may also be a reminder of the sacrificial living required of believers.

The measuring was to show that God knows, cares for and protects His Church (cf. 7:3). The worshippers were measured: God knows every one of them (2 Tim.2:19), and He cares for and protects every individual.

John was not to measure the court of the temple (11:2). Those opposed to Christ and His gospel would be allowed to trample there and in "the holy city" (cf. Dan.9:24), the sphere of Christian service. Their trampling would be limited to the court and the city. It would also be limited to forty-two months which is three-and-a-half years. It is the "time (one year), times (two years), and half a time" of Daniel 7:25 and Daniel 12:7. It is a symbol of the times when God allows the evil one and those who serve him to do their worst (cf. 12:6), but with certain limitations.

There will be those who will suffer and those whose lives will be taken by the trampling heathen. But they have been measured and their eternal security is guaranteed. That cannot be trampled.

Two Witnesses

The witnesses are described as "the two olive trees and

the two lampstands that stand before the Lord of the earth" (11:4). Continuing on the basis that this chapter is symbolic, who do these trees and lampstands symbolise?

Zechariah was shown a vision of two olive trees and a lampstand. When he asked about the olive trees he was told that they were "the two anointed ones who stand by the Lord of the whole earth" (Zech.4:14). They were symbolic of Joshua the high priest and Zerubbabel the governor.

In John's vision, the powers given to the two witnesses (11:5-6) are reminiscent of Moses and Elijah – fire (1 Kings 18:24, 28; cf. Jer.5:14), drought (1 Kings 17:1) and blood (Ex.7:20). The names of the two men are coupled together in a prophecy (Mal.4:4-5). But Jesus said that Malachi's prophecy was fulfilled in John the Baptist (Matt.11:12-14).

Zechariah saw one lampstand (Zech.4:2). John, in his first vision, was shown seven lampstands, one for each of the seven churches (1:20). In the vision of chapter 11 he was told that the witnesses were two lampstands. Perhaps they are symbolic of the two churches with which the Lord did not find fault – Smyrna (2:8-11) and Philadelphia (3:7-13). The fact that the beast "will make war on them" (11:7) certainly suggests that the "two witnesses" consist of an army rather than two individuals.

Moses and Elijah, Joshua and Zerubbabel, John the Baptist and the Lord Jesus, Smyrna and Philadelphia had this in common: they were all faithful in spite of opposition and persecution.

Dealing with the Opposition

The prophesying of the two witnesses was "a torment to those who dwell on earth" (11:10). It was torment to those who refused to repent because, for them, the message was one of condemnation (cf. 2 Cor.2:15-16). With such a solemn message it was appropriate that they should wear sackcloth (11:3).

They were to prophesy for 1,260 days. That would equate to forty-two thirty-day months. They would be preaching during the time when the nations were trampling "the holy city" (11:2) and in direct opposition to the ungodly. That and the content of their message would guarantee a hostile response. That response would not prevent the witnesses from completing their mission.

They "stand before the Lord of the earth" (11:4). They are servants of God who is Lord of all, and nothing and no-one can prevent His will being done. They are "the two olive trees". Zechariah was told that the meaning of the vision given to him (Zech.4:2-3) was a message from God to Zerubbabel. That message was, "Not by might, nor by power, but by my Spirit, says the LORD of hosts" (Zech.4:6). The two witnesses are empowered by the Holy Spirit. By Him they have special powers (11:5-6) to deal with those who seek to stop them before they have completed their mission (11:7a).

Shame and Glory

It would be the beast, the leader of mankind organised in opposition to God, who would kill the witnesses. He "rises from the bottomless pit" (11:7): he is under the influence of the evil one and gets his power from him. The ungodly will then set out to heap shame on God's servants and will seek, by doing so, to discredit them and their message.

In Old Testament times, a lack of a proper burial was considered to be a judgment from God (cf. 2 Sam.21:1-14). It is still the case in the Middle East and in many parts of the world today. The bodies of the two witnesses will be left unburied, lying in the street. The representatives of every nation (11:9) will not allow their bodies to be buried. They will be sending the message that God is judging these witnesses because they were wrong and their message may be ignored. They will have forgotten that the testimony of two witnesses is to be reckoned with (cf. Deut.19:15). Having been relieved of the torment, everybody will party, rejoice and exchange gifts in celebration of what will seem to be a great victory for evil (11:10).

This will continue for "three and a half days" (11:9). Once again this is a period of "a time, times and half a time", comparable to the forty-two months of trampling. It is the time for which God allows His servants to be disgraced, but it is relatively short. At the end of that time God breathed life into them (11:11) and called them up to heaven (11:12). They went up in a cloud as Jesus did (Acts 1:9): they were called up to glory.

The Great City

John wrote that "the great city" is called symbolically Sodom and Egypt (11:8). Sodom is a symbol of immorality. God said through Jeremiah that the people of Jerusalem had "become like Sodom to me" (Jer.23:14). Egypt is a symbol of oppression (cf. Ezek.29:6). The spiritual condition of "the great city" is like that of Sodom and Egypt.

In Revelation "the great city" is named "Babylon" (16:19; 18:16-21), the centre of mankind organised in opposition to God. To the first readers of this book this would have meant Rome. But John also says that it is "where their Lord was crucified", which would seem to mean Jerusalem.

The expression "the peoples and tribes and languages and nations" (11:9) is completely comprehensive: people of every part of the world will gaze at the bodies and refuse to allow proper burial. This seems to require more than one city. Perhaps it signifies that wherever the Lord Jesus is rejected it is as if those who reject Him crucify Him again (cf. Heb.6:6). It happens in different places and at different times in history. There may be some support for this in the way the account switches from the future (11:2-3), to the present (11:4-6), to the future (11:7-10) and then to the past (11:11-12).

Faithful Churches

The two witnesses in this chapter seem to relate to the two faithful churches of Smyrna and Philadelphia. If that is so the message may be that wherever a church is faithful to the Word of God and in holy living it will suffer opposition, persecution and even death. But the Lord will restore it to life either in the here and now or at the last day (John 6:40). There may be some support for this in the way this scene opens (11:1) - the measuring symbolises the security of the Church.

The resurrection and ascension of the witnesses will one day be fulfilled for the whole Church (1 Thess.4:17). But it has been seen to happen in the past in certain places and at certain times. The Church in China seemed to have been killed during the Boxer Uprising, but it survived and now is thriving. Following the Russian Revolution, it was decreed that God did not exist, and it seemed to the outside world that the Church there had died. But since Glasnost Russia has been open to the Gospel and the Church is thriving. There are signs that the door is beginning to close again. In many parts of the world Christians are being crushed by Islamist rulers. Perhaps someday the Church will again thrive there.

The Earthquake

The time for rewarding God's faithful servants will also be the time for judging His enemies (11:18). At the same time as the witnesses were called up to heaven, there was a great earthquake (11:13).

In the Old Testament, earthquakes are seen as demonstrations of God's power (Psa.68:8) and of His judgment (Isa.13:13). At the completion of God's plan, there will be an earthquake greater than has ever been known before (16:18) when "the great city" will be split into three, and Babylon will suffer the final judgment.

The earthquake that accompanied the witnesses' upward call was relatively mild and only one tenth of the city fell. That was merely a warning in keeping with the blowing of the trumpets. The significance of the number of 7,000 people killed is not clear.

The giving of glory to the God of heaven (11:14) was out of fear rather from any desire to serve Him.

The Three Woes

After the blowing of the fourth trumpet (8:10), John had seen an eagle. As it flew it called with a loud cry, "Woe, woe, woe to those who dwell on the earth, at the blasts of the other trumpets that the three angels are about to blow!" (8:13). It was denouncing the ungodliness and unrepentance of earth-dwellers and pronouncing judgment on them – three woes.

The passing of the first woe was declared after the blowing of the fifth trumpet (9:12), and of the second woe after the blowing of the sixth trumpet (11:14). Blowing the first four trumpets had produced damage to inanimate things only. But the blowing of the fifth and sixth trumpets had resulted in human suffering.

After the sound of the seventh trumpet and before the bowls are poured out, it was declared, "Woe to you, O earth and sea, for the devil has come down to you in great wrath, because he knows that his time is short!" (12:12). It seems to suggest that the third woe would affect the whole of creation. This proved to be the case with the pouring out of the bowls.

7. Spiritual Warfare
Revelation 12:1-17 and 13:1-18
Signs

Two signs in the sky appeared to John. In his gospel John refers to Jesus' miracles as signs. That was to say that the miracles were not simply to be enjoyed, wondered at and talked about. They had been performed in order to teach something of who Jesus is. The signs John saw have a meaning beyond their appearance.

Israel

The first sign was a woman. Since she is a sign, we should ask who she represents. There are two things that point to her identity.

One clue is in the way she was arrayed. She was clothed with the sun, the moon under her feet, and wearing a crown of twelve stars. Joseph dreamed that the sun, the moon and eleven stars bowed down to him (Gen.37:9-10). In the dream, the sun, moon and stars represented the family of Israel.

Another clue is to be found in Old Testament prophecy. Isaiah bemoaned the fact that the nation of Israel had been like a woman who had suffered the pains of childbirth but had "given birth to wind". As a nation they had "accomplished no deliverance in the earth" (Isa.26:17-18). They had failed to bring blessing to "all the families of the earth" as God had promised to Abraham (Gen.12:1-3).

But all was not lost. Micah, when prophesying that God's king would be born in Bethlehem, went on to say that this would happen "when she who is in labour has given birth" (Mic.5:2-3).

The sign that John saw was a fulfilment of all this. The woman is Israel.

The Dragon

The second sign was a red dragon. The significance of the

colour is not clear, but there is no doubt about the dragon's identity. It is "that ancient serpent, who is called the devil and Satan, the deceiver of the whole world" (12:9). The serpent is that of the Garden of Eden (Gen.3:1-5, 14-15). It is the devil, which means "the slanderer", seeking to destroy the reputation of the Church as he did that of Jesus (cf. Mark 3:22). As he deceived Eve with his lies, so he continues to deceive "the whole world".

He is Satan, the one who, before God, accuses (12:10) the people of God of faults and failings (Job 1:6; Zech.3:1). In New Testament times there were those who made their living by accusing people to the authorities.

In the Old Testament the dragon represents evil. Egypt was the epitome of oppression, and Pharaoh is referred to as "the great dragon" (Ezek.29:3; cf. Isa.51:9-10). God promised that in the day when he will restore His people, He will "slay the dragon that is in the sea" (Isa.27:1). That is to say that He will destroy all evil.

The dragon seen by John had seven heads. This probably signifies that it would be hard to kill. Cut off one head but it still has another six. It had ten horns. The horn was a symbol of power. This dragon wields great power. He wears seven diadems, exercising unlimited influence over those he controls.

With his tail he swept down one third of the stars (12:4). This was merely a show of strength intended to intimidate. His main purpose was to devour the child the moment the woman gave birth.

The Man Child

If the woman is Israel, it follows that the child born to her (12:5) is God's king, the Christ, who is Jesus. He is to "rule the nations with a rod of iron." Literally it means that He is to rule as a shepherd. The rod of iron in New Testament times signified, not tyranny but firmness.

From birth His life was threatened, first by Herod then constantly by the religious leaders. Then He was crucified but rose again. None of these details is shown in the sign John saw. The whole story is condensed into His birth and ascension. None of the attempts to destroy Him was successful – "her child was caught up to God and his throne".

Behind the threats to the life of Jesus was the dragon. The reference to God's throne is to emphasise that, in spite of the dragon's apparent invincibility, God is in control all the time.

The Battle in Heaven

"Now war arose in heaven" when Michael and his angels attacked the dragon and his angels (12:7). Michael is described in Daniel as "one of the chief princes" (Dan.10:13), and Daniel was told that he is "the great prince who has charge of your people" (Dan.12:1).

The war resulted in victory for Michael and his angels. The dragon and his angels were defeated. They were thrown out of heaven and down to earth.

Jesus told His disciples, "I saw Satan fall like lightning from heaven" (Luke 10:18). That is often taken to refer to what He saw before He became man. But it may require a different meaning.

For one thing, as He approached the Cross, Jesus said, "*Now* will the ruler of this world be cast out" (John 12:31). Also, the phrase of two words with which 12:7 begins, and which the ESV translates "Now", suggests that the war in heaven followed on immediately from what John has recorded in the first six verses. And it is clear in verses 10 and 11 that Satan's defeat and the Cross, "the blood of the Lamb", are closely linked.

The Battle on Earth

The defeat of the dragon is cause for great rejoicing for those who dwell in the heavens (12:12). This means all believers, since God has raised us up to sit "in the heavenly places in Christ Jesus" (Eph.2:6; cf. Col.3:1-3). They rejoice because the one who was free to accuse them before God (cf. Job 1:6-12) has been thrown down (12:12). "The salvation and the power and the kingdom of our God and the authority of his Christ" are fully evident (12:10).

The devil has been thrown down to earth. Believers still have a personal battle to fight against the forces of evil (Eph.6:10-18). Victory is gained "by the blood of the Lamb and by the word of their testimony" (12:11). That is to say, by trusting in the victory Christ won at the Cross and by being faithful to Him even at the cost of their lives (Luke 14:26).

For those who dwell on earth, that is, for those who have refused to repent and accept Christ, it is "woe" (12:12). They will experience God's judgment. The devil has been let loose among them. He is in a great rage, hitting out in spite, because "he knows that his time is short". He is seeking to do all the damage he can in the time he has left.

The Church

The dragon's first target was the woman (12:13). She is Israel, not the nation of descendants of Abraham, Isaac and Jacob (cf. Rom.9:6), but the true Israel, "the Israel of God" (Gal.6:16), those who, whether Jew or Gentile, belong to Christ (Gal.3:28-29). This is the Church.

The Church is under God's protection in a place prepared for her. She will be provided for during the 1,260 days of her witness (11:3; 12:14). This will be "in the wilderness", a reminder of God's provision of manna for the Israelites during their wanderings, and of bread and meat for Elijah in the years of drought (1 Kings 17:1-7). It is also a reminder of the fact that this world is not where the Church belongs. "Our citizenship is in heaven" (Phil.3:20). Every believer can say in the words of the old spiritual, "This world is not my home, I'm just a-passing through."

The serpent's attempts to pursue and destroy the Church failed. She was given the wings of an eagle with which she could easily outpace him. He tried to overwhelm her with evil (12:15). But, just as the Red sea parted and the Hebrews crossed on dry land (Ex.14:21-22), so the earth absorbed the devil's flood (12:16; cf. Ex.15:12).

Having been frustrated in his attempts to destroy the Church as a whole, the devil went off to attack individual believers (12:17). He would do that through secular and religious leaders who give themselves over to his control.

The Beast from the Sea

John saw a beast rise out of the sea (13:1). The dragon was standing on the seashore (12:17) as if summoning up the beast. In ancient times the sea was always seen as being evil or a symbol of evil (cf. Isa.27:1) in that it was untameable and unpredictable.

Like its master the dragon, it had ten horns and seven heads. Unlike the dragon, it had ten diadems and these were on its horns. Perhaps the meaning is that, whereas the devil exerts his influence by cunning, the beast exerts his by brute force.

An Evil Beast

In a vision Daniel had seen four beasts, one like a lion, one like a bear, one like a leopard, and another with ten horns which Daniel could describe only as "terrifying and dreadful and exceedingly strong" (Dan.7:2-7). The beast that John saw seems to be an amalgamation of all four.

It had seven heads but only one mouth. This seems impossible, but the beast was evidently so horrible that John struggled to describe it. It represented evil beyond the limits of human imagination.

The unimaginable evil of it was because the dragon gave it "his power and his throne and great authority" (13:2). It had all the power of the devil but not all his authority. It remained under the domination of the devil.

A Blasphemous Beast

On its head it had "blasphemous names". All its thoughts, wishes and plans were in opposition to God and insulted Him. It blasphemed God's name (13:6), that is, it blasphemed everything about God. It blasphemed "His dwelling", that is, those in whom God dwells.

The worst blasphemy was that it enticed the world into worshipping it. They did this for two reasons. One was that it had a wound that seemed to be fatal and yet it had survived (13:3). The other reason was that the beast was so brutal that they were afraid to refuse (13:4). What the world probably did not realise was that in worshipping the beast they were in fact worshipping the dragon (13:4) who is the devil.

Suffering but Secure

The beast was allowed to attack and kill the saints (13:7), those who are Christ's. They have nothing to fear from the beast because their names are written in the Lamb's book of life (13:8).

Whether this verse means that their names were written (ESV, ASV), or that the Lamb was killed (KJV, NIV) "before the foundation of the world", matters not at all. Both are true (Eph.1:4; 1 Pet.1:19-20). Their salvation and eternal security is something that God determined before time began. Their names are written in the book and they will never be forgotten.

The Beast's Identity

To the first readers of this book it would have seemed obvious that this beast represented the Roman emperor. The empire was ruled by brute force. Some of their ways of administering justice were horrific. Crucifixes were a common sight, and that was the fate that many Christians suffered under Domitian. To Christians the blasphemy of some of the Roman emperors was obvious in that they had demanded to be honoured as gods. But one empire and one line of rulers does not meet the case.

The beast had suffered a fatal wound and yet had lived. The problem was that it had been "wounded by the sword" (13:14). The point is that evil cannot be destroyed by war or by any other human means. It may appear to have been destroyed but it will rise again at another time and in other people. It is the dragon who calls them up and empowers them and, until he is thrown into the lake of fire, he will continue to do so.

For all the brutality of Roman rulers and the harshness of their rule, the beast from the sea seems to surpass them all. This passage probably points forward to a time in the last days when there will be an outbreak of extreme evil. Paul wrote of a time of rebellion when "the man of lawlessness" will be revealed. Paul called him "the son of destruction" who would even sit "in the temple of God" and would proclaim himself to be God (2 Thess.2:3-4). It will be as if Satan had taken human form!

The Beast from the Earth

A second beast arose that seemed far less threatening than the first. For one thing it rose out of the earth (13:11). The earth is something that people were familiar with. For one thing, they used it to produce food. The beast had only two horns like a lamb. It did speak "like a dragon", but this may mean that it had the devil's persuasive and deceitful way of speaking. It certainly deceived people by the magic signs it performed (13:14). These included bringing fire down from heaven (cf. 1 Kings 18:24), and by bringing to life the image of the first beast which it had told the people to make (13:14-15).

The inhabitants of earth were evidently in great awe of the first beast because it had survived a fatal wound (13:12, 14), and the second beast speaks with all the authority of the first beast. It does so "in its presence", not in opposition but by combining their forces. By this and by all other deceitful means it persuades the world to worship the first beast and its image (13:12, 15).

The Identity of the Second Beast

Satan uses people to do his evil work. The first beast represents the secular world leader who is under the devil's control. The second beast represents the religious world leader. It is "the false prophet" (16:13; 19:20; 20:10).

The first readers of this book would have seen in the second beast a symbol of the chief priest of the Roman cultic priesthood. Some emperors took the title of chief priest for themselves and promoted themselves as gods. But mostly the Roman chief priests performed the religious rites required by the Roman deities.

The extreme measures which the second beast adopts indicate something more serious than a Roman chief priest. Paul wrote that the coming of "the lawless one" would be "by the activity of Satan with all power and false signs and wonders, and with all wicked deception" (2 Thess.2:9-10). God will send to the world in the last days "a strong delusion so that they may believe what is false" (2 Thess.2:11).

With Permission

The dragon is certainly powerful (12:3-4). The first beast is so powerful that the people of earth think that it would be futile to fight against it (13:4). The second beast seems to be able to deceive the whole world (13:14). But they all are able to do only what God allows them to do.

The dragon is unable to destroy either the man child or His mother. He has been defeated and thrown down from heaven. His time on earth is short. The day will come when he will be thrown into the lake of fire (20:10).

The first beast was *allowed* to exercise authority for forty-two months (13:5). This means during the time for which the nations are allowed to trample the holy city (11:2). It was *allowed* to attack and kill the saints and *given authority* over the whole world (13:7-8). The second beast was *allowed* to do magic signs (13:14) and was *allowed* to bring to life the image of the first beast (13:15). Both beasts will be captured and thrown into the lake of fire (19:20).

Imitations

The first beast mimics the resurrection of Jesus by displaying a fatal wound which it has survived (13:3; cf. 5:6).

The worship the first beast draws from the world is expressed by, "Who is like the beast, and who can fight against it?" (13:4). It is mimicking the words addressed to God in the Song of Moses (Ex.15:11) and the words of David (Psa.35:10). The name of the great prince who defeated the dragon is probably significant as a rebuke to those who worship the beast: Michael means "Who is like God?"

The second beast "had two horns like a lamb" in imitation of the Lamb who is worthy of all "power and wealth and wisdom and might and honour and glory and blessing" (5:12). The second beast is the *false* prophet, an imitation prophet.

People are deceived by these imitations because they have rejected the truth (2 Thess.2:10-12).

The Mark

The beast from the earth causes everyone without exception to be marked in a conspicuous place. Anyone without this mark would be barred from buying and selling.

That would make survival impossible.

The mark may be to indicate ownership or an acceptance of the beast's authority. It would prove that the one bearing the mark was a faithful follower of the beast.

The mark is the number 666 (13:18). In Hebrew and Greek, letters were used to represent numbers. Most English versions have "it is the number of a man". The number 666 may be code for a name. Attempts have been made to discover what that name might be. Even from the time when Revelation was first being circulated, there has been no agreement about the meaning.

In Greek the first nine letters of the alphabet were used to represent the numbers 1 to 9, the second nine letters represented 10, 20 ... 90, the third nine 100, 200 ... 900, and so on. The values of the letters of the name Jesus in Greek (Ἰησοῦς) are as follows: Ι = 10; η = 8; σ = 200; ο = 70; υ = 400; ς = 200. The sum of the values of the letters is 888. Seven is the number of perfection, so each digit in the sum of the letters of Jesus' name is one more than perfection.

Since the indefinite article does not appear in the phrase in Rev.13:18, it could be translated "the number of man". In 666 each digit is one less than perfection. Everything that a human being does is tainted by sin (Isa.64:6).

Bearing that mark could mean an acceptance of man's fallen state and of sinful living, and a rejection of God's offer of salvation. Anyone who accepted Christ and set out to live for Him could not bear the mark and would be an outcast. This is what many Muslims who accept Christ suffer in these days.

The Call

Jesus said that the aim of false christs and false prophets would be to try to lead astray even believers (Mark 13:22). John calls the attention of the seven churches to what he is reporting of these visions. He uses a saying which he had heard Jesus use, "If anyone has an ear, let him hear" (13:9).

Jesus used the words to get His hearers to think carefully about what He had already said. John may be doing that, but he may be calling attention especially to what he was about to write (13:10).

Being faithful to Christ may mean imprisonment or even death. Christians have to endure these things while maintaining their faith in the fact that their eternal well-being is in the hands of their Father in heaven. The second part of the verse may be a warning not to use force to defend themselves against persecution (cf. Matt.26:52).

"Here is a call for the endurance and faith of the saints."

8. Harvest Time

Revelation 14:1-20

The chapter could be understood as beginning with a vision of the Church, finally secure with Christ, and continuing with a summary of the events leading up to that state.

The Church

It seemed clear that the 144,000 which John heard had been sealed (7:4) referred to the multitude which he saw (7:9) and was the Church. It would seem reasonable to assume that the same applies to the 144,000 here (14:1). However, there is an apparent problem with that assumption.

It is said that they "have not defiled themselves with women, for they are virgins" (14:4). This would seem to indicate that they are all men. However, describing men as "virgins" did not occur in New Testament times. In addition, the New Testament does not teach that sexual relations within marriage is defiling. Paul taught that husband and wife should not deprive one another of their conjugal rights (1 Cor.7:3-5), and that forbidding to marry will occur "in later times" by those who "will depart from the faith" (1 Tim.4:1-5). It is commanded that "marriage be held in honour among all". It is immorality and adultery that defile the marriage bed (Heb.13:4).

The statement in Revelation is symbolic. In the Old Testament, God speaks of Himself as Israel's husband (Hos.2:16), and worshipping pagan gods is spoken of in terms of prostitution and adultery (Jer.3:6-9). In the New Testament, the Church is described as Christ's bride (Rev.19:7-8, 21:9). Paul, writing of the time when he had led the Corinthians to Christ, said "I betrothed you to one husband, to present you as a pure virgin to Christ" (2 Cor.11:2). He had become concerned that they would be "led astray from a sincere and pure devotion to Christ" when some came preaching a different gospel (2 Cor.11:3-4).

Those standing with the Lamb on Mount Zion (14:1) have kept themselves separate from the heathen ways of the world. Typical of those ways is to lie (14:5) with the purpose of gaining advantage over another. But these have "put on the new self" (Col.3:9-10). They "follow the Lamb wherever He goes" (14:4). His way is the way of truth (1 Pet.2:21-22).

Mount Zion

Mount Zion is where "the LORD of hosts dwells" (Isa.8:18). Among promises of restoration of His people, God says that there shall be a day when the call will come, "Arise, and let us go up to Zion, to the LORD our God" (Jer.31:6). There God has set His King (Psa.2:6) and there He will reign over His people forever (Mic.4:7).

It is a place of security: the dragon stands on sand (12:17), but the Lamb stands on Mount Zion (14:1). Those who worship the beast bear his mark of ownership (13:16). On earth the 144,000 were sealed for protection with "the seal of the living God" (7:2-4). Now they are in heaven bearing the names of the Lamb and of the Father. Not one has been lost (John 10:27-29), they are safe forever.

A New Song

The 144,000 were singing a song (14:3) in God's presence. They were singing with a voice like their Saviour's (1:15), a voice that was as loud as thunder yet as sweet as the sound of harps (14:2). They were singing in harmony with Jesus, with great enthusiasm and with great enjoyment.

It was a new song. It was not mere repetition of words written by someone else. It was sung spontaneously from the heart in response to what had been done for them (cf. Psa.33:3; Isa.42:10). They had been "redeemed", set free from sin's slavery by the life of Jesus given for them (Mark 10:45). They are "first-fruits", the exclusive property of God and the

Lamb (14:4; Jas.1:18; cf. Ex.23:19; Neh.10:35-37; Prov.3:9). Their song is new in the sense that only the redeemed can sing it.

The Final Call

Before the redeemed had been brought to stand with the Lamb on Mount Zion, a final call had been made to the world. This had been brought by three angels "flying directly overhead" (14:6), visible to all, so that no-one could say that they had not heard.

The first angel came with a gospel that was valid for eternity and was for everybody without exception. It was a reminder that God is the Creator of all things (14:7). He has real power in contrast to that of the beast whose power had been given it by the dragon. Because of Who God is, the world is called upon to fear Him, to give Him reverent obedience. The world is called upon to give Him glory, to acknowledge His greatness in thought, word and deed. The world is called upon to worship Him by giving themselves as living sacrifices (cf. Rom.12:1-2).

The opportunity for responding to this call will soon be gone because "the hour of His judgment has come" (14:7).

The Caution

The second angel came with the message that Babylon is fallen (14:8).

At the time John had this vision Babylon had been deserted for more than two hundred years. The name Babylon is a "name of mystery" (Rev.17:5). It means something other than the ruined city of that name.

"Babylon" is the Greek version of the Mesopotamian name "Babel". The first mention of it in the Bible is in Genesis 11:1-9. It is so common to speak of the tower of Babel that it is often forgotten that the people of that day said, "Let us build ourselves a city ..." (Gen.11:4). Their purpose in building the city and the tower was to make a name for themselves as opposed to bringing honour to the LORD's name. God intervened and the city was left unfinished (Gen.11:8).

Babel or Babylon is a symbol of the spirit that entices man to organise himself against God. In Jeremiah's time Babel was the ruling spirit in Babylon (Jer.51:6-7), in Ezekiel's time it was in Tyre and in John's time it was in Rome (Rev.17:9). It is the ruling spirit of every Godless empire, past, present and future. Just as the sexual purity of the redeemed is symbolic of their faithful devotion to Christ, so the "sexual immorality" of Babylon is symbolic of the heathen, Godless influence of that ruling spirit.

The angel announced, "Fallen, fallen is Babylon the great". The repetition means that the outcome is certain.

Consequences

Those who follow her lead in worshipping the beast will fall with her.

The image of the cup of wrath occurs again in 15:7 (cf. Isa.51:17, 22-23; cf. Ezek.23:32-34). For the worshippers of the beast it will be "poured full strength" (14:10). Having rejected God's final call of grace, they will experience the full force of God's anger (Psa.75:8). While the "fire and sulphur" are symbolic, they represent a most painful experience. It is a torment that goes on forever and from which there will be no relief (14:11).

In their martyrdom, Christians provided entertainment for their persecutors. In the final judgment, those who tortured them will suffer in the presence, not of those who take a delight in what they see, but of those who are there to see that justice is done. They are the *holy* angels and the Lamb.

A Call for Endurance

In view of this, believers should take care that they are not led astray through fear of the beast or by being deceived

(13:14). The call for them is, "Hang on!" Giving up and accepting the mark of the beast to escape persecution will result in suffering the fate prescribed for worshippers of the beast.

This requires endurance in keeping "the commandments of God and their faith in Jesus" (14:12) even to the point of death. In fact, those who "die in the Lord" are blessed, even though they are dead. God will bless them with real happiness, with a joy that the world can never give.

The Spirit confirms this pronouncement. He says that the blessedness will come because, in the life to come, their work will go on, but without the hard labour that they have experienced on earth.

Heaven is evidently not an experience of idleness!

The Harvest of the Redeemed

Some see difficulties with identifying the figure he saw on the cloud (14:14) with the risen Christ. The command given by the angel who came out of the temple is very abrupt for one addressing Christ. The Lord would be shown apparently doing a similar job to a mere angel (14:17-19), the one who reaps the grape harvest. It is also thought strange that the Lamb on the throne still does not know that "the hour to reap has come" (cf. Mark 13:32; Acts 1:7).

There are several points which support identifying this figure with Christ. In his vision, Daniel saw "one like a son of man" coming "with the clouds of heaven" (Dan.7:13). The churches to which this writing was sent would have known Daniel's prophecy and we might expect them to assume that the figure that John saw (14:14) was Christ. They would probably have thought that this was confirmed by the fact that he wore a golden crown. They would probably have been familiar with Paul's teaching that, at the rapture, "the Lord himself" will come to take His people to be with Him

(1 Thess.4:16-18).

There are two distinct harvests in this vision. If the "one like a son of man" is Christ then the first harvest is of the redeemed (cf. Mark 4:29). Of this harvest the angel says that "the harvest of the earth is fully ripe" (14:15). The word for "ripe" is used to describe grain that has turned white and so is ready to harvest (cf. John 4:35).

"The hour to reap has come." When the time had come God sent His Son (Gal.4:4). When the time had come Jesus went to the Cross (John 17:1). Everything has been planned, everything is under God's control. In God's own time the Lord will come to take His people home. The One who sat on the cloud swung His sickle and the earth was reaped (14:16). His sickle is sharp, none will be left behind.

The Harvest of the Unrepentant

There is no doubt about the identity of the reaper of this harvest. He is an angel (14:17). Jesus said that he would send His angels to remove from His kingdom all that is evil (Matt.13:41). John saw the angel coming "out of the temple in heaven". He came from the presence of God and the Lamb and at His command.

The angel who gave the command to reap "came out from the altar" (14:18). The altar is linked with the prayers of saints and with the just judgment and vindication for which they pray (8:3-5). This angel is the one who has authority over the fire which was thrown on the earth in response to the saints' prayers (8:5).

His command to the angel with the sickle was to use his sickle because the harvest is ripe (14:18). His sickle is sharp so that none will escape God's judgment.

The picture of using a sickle to reap grapes seems strange, but it occurs in the Old Testament. There the grape harvest is a time for decision (Joel 3:12-14). The people of the earth, those who have so far refused to repent, are called to be given the last chance to repent (14:6-11). When that is rejected the sickle is swung and the grapes are reaped.

In stark contrast to the destiny of the grain harvest, the grapes are thrown into "the great winepress of the wrath of God" (14:19). Christ Himself will "tread the grapes" (cf. Isa.63:1-6). He is the one God has appointed to judge the world (Acts 17:30-31).

The winepress "was trodden outside the city" (14:20). This is the place of rejection, the place where the rubbish was thrown. It was where the Son of God, scorned and rejected by sinful men, suffered and died. In the last judgment, those who have persisted in their rejection of God's Saviour, will themselves be finally rejected.

The distance for which the blood flowed is symbolic. 1,600 is the product of 4^2 and 10^2. 4 is the number of earth and 10 is the number of completeness. The final judgment, the judgment of the whole earth will be complete. It will be the end of all evil.

We shy away from the thought of so much blood and of these demonstrations of the wrath of God. We prefer to think of Him as a God of love. But the purpose for which Jesus came "was to destroy the works of the devil" (Heb.2:14; 1 John 3:8). Without the destruction of evil our salvation would be short-lived and ineffective.

9. The End of Human Opposition
Revelation 17:1 to 19:5
Identity

The seven bowls are the outpouring of God's final judgment on all that is opposed to Him (16:1-21). It was, therefore, fitting that one of the angels who "had the seven bowls" should come to John to show him "the judgment of the great prostitute" (17:1).

John was taken to see a woman sitting on a scarlet beast (17:3). Her name is "Babylon the great" (17:5), that "name of mystery" which signifies more than merely the city of that name. The most obvious way for John's readers to understand this would have been to see it as a reference to Rome. The seven heads of the beast "are seven mountains on which the woman is seated" (17:9). The city of Rome is built on seven hills. The waters on which the woman is seated represent "peoples and multitudes and nations and languages" (17:15), the Roman empire (cf. 17:18).

But Rome could not be held responsible for the deaths of all prophets and saints, certainly not of "all who have been slain on earth" (18:24). And "the great" indicates that John is being shown the final consummation of all the incarnations of the spirit of Babylon under which influence humanity organises itself in opposition to God.

Eyes Opened

The angel said, "I will show you the judgment of the great prostitute", but this does not take place immediately. First John must realise how evil Babylon is.

To understand this, he had to be "in the Spirit" (17:3), that is, he had to be completely taken up with spiritual realities to the exclusion of earthly things. The best place for that was to be in "a wilderness", away from the city and all its allure, where he could appreciate an objective view.

When John saw what she was really like he "marvelled greatly" (17:6). The angel's reaction to John's amazement (17:7) suggests that John should have been aware of how evil she is.

The Great Prostitute

In the OT, prostitution is used as a symbol of idolatry (Je.3:9), or of the effects of such pagan worship on daily life.

Isaiah wrote that the people of Jerusalem, "the faithful city", had forsaken God's ways and had "become a whore" (Isa.1:21). The secular leaders are described as "rebels and companions of thieves" (Isa.1:23). The judges were taking bribes and, as a result, the rights of orphans and widows were being ignored. Everything that was good in their society had been ruined (Isa.1:22).

God said through the prophet Hosea that "the land commits great whoredom by forsaking the LORD" (Hos.1:2). The people were worshipping Baal because they believed that that was the way to ensure that they had enough food, drink and all material things (Hos.2:5).

That is what the great prostitute shown to John is all about. She convinces people that by following heathen ways and pagan worship they will enjoy material prosperity. It is the same deception that was practised on Eve (Gen.3:6).

This is "the great prostitute", the consummation of every manifestation of prostitution. She gives birth to prostitutes (17:5) in order that her dominion may be an empire of prostitution.

False Promises

The woman was colourfully and richly clothed (17:4). Purple was a costly dye and purple garments were worn by royalty (Judg.8:26) and by those a ruler wished to honour (Est.8:15). Jesus was clothed in purple (Mark 15:16-20), or scarlet (Matt.27:27-31), in mockery of His claim to be a king.

She was lavishly adorned in gold, jewels and pearls. She was decked out like a queen (cf. 18:7). All of this was to demonstrate her respectability and her ability to confer honour and blessings on those who came to her. In the same way the cup of gold would promise a satisfying drink and would entice earth-dwellers to come to her.

But it was a total deception. In spite of her royal attire she was a prostitute – the great prostitute. The cup was "filled with the filthy and nasty things she had done" (17:4 CEV). The word which the majority of English versions translate as "abominations" (17:4), is used in the Old Testament for idolatry and the immoral practices associated with it (Lev.18:20-28). It is the prostitute's purpose to fill the whole world with these things (17:5).

Rome was the place of influence, it was there that the emperors showed off their wealth and power, "all roads led to Rome", and citizens of the empire were proud of her. But the Roman philosopher Seneca, who had been Nero's tutor then advisor, called Rome "a filthy sewer".

For all her attractive appearance, this woman is a killer. She not only purposes to fill the earth with evil but she is out to destroy those who uphold Godliness (17:6). Instead of "the blood of the saints" making her sick, she has become drunk on it. She enjoys the killing.

She has succeeded in that she has seduced "the kings of the earth" (17:2). No doubt world rulers would be convinced that following her ways was politically advantageous and would guarantee their nations' and their own prosperity. They have been drawn into policies and practices that are opposed to God and His laws. Their people "have become drunk" on the apparent advantages of living in Godless ways. Becoming "drunk" probably carries the idea of becoming addicted. They have no desire to be sober and would be helpless to break the addiction.

The Beast

The woman was sitting on a scarlet beast that "was full of blasphemous names" and with seven heads and ten horns (17:3). This is the beast that John saw rising out of the sea (13:1-8). It is unimaginably evil and has all the power of the devil (13:2). It attacks and kills the saints (13:7). Being "full" of blasphemous names means that it could not be more opposed to God and His ways. This is the secular leader of mankind organised in opposition to God.

The great prostitute rides on this beast. There is only one mystery of the woman and the beast (17:7). The woman is completely at one with the beast in purpose and direction. The beast uses her to entice the world to worship him (13:4; 17:2) and thus to follow his lead.

The first time John saw the beast it had a mortal wound in one of its seven heads (13:3). But that wound was healed as if the beast had come back to life. In the explanation of "the mystery", John is told that the beast "was, and is not, and is about to rise from the bottomless pit" (17:8).

There was a belief that Nero would return to life after his death in 68 AD. It was thought by many that Domitian, the emperor in power at the time of Revelation, was a fulfilment of that. To those who believed this, the apparent resurrection was a great marvel and an incentive to worship Domitian (cf. 13:3). What they did not realise was that the beast would not last forever but will "go to destruction" (17:8, 11).

There have been many manifestations and revivals of the beast. One day, secular leadership of mankind organised in opposition to God will be destroyed forever.

Jesus is able to say, "I died, and behold I am alive for evermore" (1:18). He is the one to follow.

The Seven Heads
The seven heads "are seven mountains" (17:9) but "they are also seven kings" (17:10). Five of those kings are already dead, one of them is in power, and the seventh will reign for a short time (17:10). It is impossible to be certain of the identity of these "kings".

One suggestion is that the churches to which John wrote would have most readily understood these to be Roman emperors. It is held that the first would be Augustus and the fifth Nero. The sixth would then be Galba and the seventh Otho. But the latter died in 69 AD. So many scholars leave out Galba, Otho and Vitellius. No explanation is given as to why John and his readers would have done the same. It is then suggested that Vespasian is the sixth and Titus the seventh.

But if Revelation was written during the reign of Domitian (who followed Titus), one would expect that John and his readers would regard him as the sixth "king", the one who "is".

Another suggestion is that the seven heads represent seven kingdoms. It is said that the five that have fallen would be Ancient Babylonia, Assyria, New Babylonia, Medo-Persia, and Greco-Macedonia. Rome is the one at the time of writing Revelation. All these empires were opposed to God and His ways. The word "only" is supplied by the ESV. If that is omitted, the emphasis, it is said, falls on "remain". The seventh empire is then seen to be the summation of all organised opposition to God since Rome. It is held that Daniel's interpretation of Nebuchadnezzar's dream (Dan.2) and Daniel's dream of four beasts (Dan.7) support this explanation.

Perhaps trying to identify these "kings" is the wrong approach or, at best, only part of the solution. Seven may once again be a symbol of completeness. In that case the comforting thing for John and his readers would be that God knows in detail the whole history of human opposition to Him. Any emperor or empire that comes to a reader's mind is simply an example of the outworking of the spirit of Babylon. Nothing in the way of opposition or persecution has ever happened or will happen without God's knowledge.

These seven are manifestations of the beast (17:11). For the second time John is told that the beast "goes to destruction". God will bring to a complete end all opposition to Him, to His ways and to His people.

The Ten Horns

As with the seven kings, there are difficulties in interpreting the ten (17:12). From John's standpoint they are in the future. The statement that they will have authority for one hour may mean that they are of very little significance, certainly as far as God is concerned.

There are several indications that they may be demonic rather than human. They will rule with the beast and will be "of one mind" with it (17:13). They will make futile war on the Lamb (17:14). They, with the beast, will carry out God's purposes by turning on the prostitute and destroying her (17:16-17; cf. 18:2). On the other hand, the human kings of the earth will mourn the destruction of the prostitute which is the great city (17:18; 18:9).

Appropriate Punishment

John then saw an angel who came from God's presence (18:1), with God's authority, with God's glory (cf. Ezek.43:2) and with a voice of power. What he was about to say must surely happen. "Fallen, fallen is Babylon the great!" (18:2). It is as good as done.

Her fall will be brought about by her hosting demons and every possible kind of thing which is spiritually unclean (cf. Isa.13:19-22). No doubt she has, by her immoral behaviour, invited these things in. The reason for her condemnation is that she has brought about the corruption of others (18:3).

"Her sins are heaped high as heaven" as a constant reminder to God. She will not get away with anything (Rom.2:3-6; Gal.6:7). She will be repaid double for what she has dealt out to others (18:6). Paying back and repaying have the sense of paying what has been earned (cf. Rom.6:23). This is not a question of revenge but of a measured and appropriate response to her sins. The extent of her Godless self-glorification and her worship of material things will receive "a like measure of torment and weeping" (18:7). For the mighty Lord God this will be the work of "a single day" (18:8), of one sweep of His right arm.

The Call to Come Out

When God's people are suffering persecution and oppression because of their faith, it is a great temptation to come to terms with the authorities, to modify lifestyle so as to blend in, to keep quiet about beliefs and the wrongs in society, or even to recant. Such responses can bring an end to persecution and poverty. But John and his readers and all God's people throughout history need to know how evil Babylon is, what her fate will be, and that those who link themselves with her will also suffer the same fate.

God's call to His people is, "Come out of her, my people, lest you take part in her sins, lest you share in her plagues" (18:4). This has always been God's call to His people. Jeremiah appealed to the exiles in Babylon to "flee from the midst of Babylon" because of God's impending judgment on Babylon through invasion (Jer.50:8-9). At the time of the prophecy the exiles would not have been free to leave. But they were being warned that, when the time came, they should escape with their lives (Jer.51:6, 45). A similar call comes to Christians not to get so closely involved in the world system that they find themselves manoeuvred off the narrow way (2 Cor.6:14-18).

Lamentations and Rejoicing

At the destruction of the great city, there will be no mourning for the city itself. Those who mourn will do so because of what they lose by her passing. The kings will mourn because Babylon was a "mighty city" (18:10). She was their source of power through which they enjoyed their obscene luxuries.

For example, Vitellius was emperor for five months in 69 AD. He was described by the historian Suetonius as lazy and self-indulgent, fond of eating and drinking. He was an obese glutton, eating banquets four times a day. He feasted on rare foods he would send the Roman navy to procure. Meanwhile, the poor of the empire starved.

The merchants and the merchant seamen mourn because "no-one buys their cargo" (18:11), because all the wealth has been "laid waste" (18:17), and because they will no longer be able to make themselves rich (18:19).

The enormity of their loss is emphasised by the long list of the goods in which they traded (18:12-13). The Godlessness of their trade is hammered home by the last item on the list – "slaves, that is, human souls".

Everyone will keep their distance (18:10, 15, 17), wanting to avoid being involved in the city's destruction. No doubt they will be hoping that they will survive to find another way to continue their Godless pursuit of power and wealth. God tells them that they will never get it back (18:14). When Babylon is removed, all such pursuit of power and wealth will cease.

Kings, merchants and seamen will all exclaim that the end has come "in a single hour" (18:10, 17, 19). The fall from great power and wealth to nothing will come "in no time at all", and they will all be in shock.

For the "saints, apostles and prophets" it will be time a

time for rejoicing (18:20). Judgment will have been given in their favour. God will be showing that everything that they had proclaimed and had lived and died for was right. The way to lasting pleasure and wealth is to follow Jesus Christ.

Buried Without Trace

The final pronouncement of the judgment to come is that Babylon will disappear without trace. This is illustrated by a mighty angel throwing "a stone like a great millstone" into the sea (18:21). A millstone tied round a person's neck and thrown into the sea would be enough to prevent them rising to the surface (Matt.18:6). They would be held down forever. Similarly, Babylon will never be seen again.

Nothing of her will survive. Normal, day-to-day activities will cease: celebrations, daily work and the preparation of food (18:22). All signs of life will disappear: there will be no-one to light a lamp or to get married (18:23).

The reason for Babylon's punishment is that she deceived the whole world (18:23) into thinking that by following her they would gain lasting wealth and satisfaction (cf. 1 Tim.6:17).

Babylon Today

The great prostitute, the spirit of Babylon, lives on. The day when she is thrown out to disappear without trace is yet to come. But there is probably general ignorance among Christians today about the evils and dangers to spiritual life of becoming too closely involved in the world system. The pressures to compromise are great in every area of life.

At the time of writing Christian bakers are going through the courts. They are having to defend their refusal to bake a cake decorated in a way that promotes gay marriage.

A department of the government is doing its utmost to sexualise children through education. If these efforts are successful, the next generation will be completely amoral.

Christians working in health and justice have lost their

jobs through insisting that the Biblical view of the family is right and is best for the children.

The spirit of Babylon exerts its influence in the lives of individuals. The need to earn enough to pay the bills and provide food and shelter for oneself and one's dependants can easily develop into a seeking after wealth for its own sake. Then money takes God's place and Christian principles and values are abandoned. The great prostitute has achieved her purpose.

"Godliness with contentment is great gain" (1 Tim.6:6-8; Heb.13:5).

10. Celebrations

Revelation 19:1-21

A Celebration of God's Justice

John then heard the heavenly host crying out, "Hallelujah!" (19:1) This is a transliteration of a Hebrew word meaning "praise God". They praise Him because "salvation and glory and power belong to Him", that is, they are His and His alone. This is emphasised by the repetition of the word "throne" in verse 4 and 5. "Hallelujah! For the Lord our God the almighty reigns" (19:6).

They praise God because His judgments are true and just (19:2). This has been demonstrated in the destruction of Babylon, the great prostitute. She deserved her punishment because she had corrupted the whole world and had killed God's servants.

They praise God because the smoke from her burning will be everlasting evidence of God's justice. It will also provide a perpetual reminder of the folly of opposing God and enticing others to do the same.

The heavenly host is joined in worship by the twenty-four elders, representing the Church, and by the four living creatures, representing creation (19:4). Then a voice, speaking with all God's authority, calls on all who fear God, all who submit to His will and seek to serve Him, to join in the praise and worship (19:5).

Inescapable Justice

Two British men left the UK and went to join an Islamist group. They tortured and shot or beheaded more than one hundred Christians. They were captured and are now in prison awaiting trial. Because their British citizenship has been revoked, it is uncertain who should conduct the trial. Relatives are concerned that in the midst of all the uncertainty these men will escape justice.

Many wicked people have escaped justice in this life. But before the great white throne (20:11-15) detailed records will be consulted and justice administered.

A Celebration of a Wedding

That it is once again heavenly beings that are rejoicing is shown by the fact that John, in describing what he heard, uses the phrase "what seemed to be" and "like" twice (19:6). Heaven is rejoicing because God has shown that He reigns in that "the marriage of the Lamb has come" (19:7).

There are a number of times in the Bible when the relationship between God and His people is described in marital terms (e.g. Isa.54:5; Hos.2:16). John the Baptist explained to his disciples that the reason he must fade out and give place to Jesus was because He, Jesus is the bridegroom (John 3:26-30). Jesus also referred to Himself as the bridegroom (Matt.9:14-15).

The fulfilment of that relationship in marriage is yet to take place. Invitations have been issued; the bride has made herself ready. For now, the Church is betrothed to Christ (2 Cor.11:2). But in New Testament times a betrothal, an engagement was as binding as marriage (cf. Matt.1:18-19). The betrothal of the Church to Christ is for ever (cf. Hos.2:19-20). The sealing of the Holy Spirit as a guarantee could be seen as a sort of engagement ring. God keeps His promises, and John was told that the marriage of the Lamb had come.

Being Ready

Because the marriage is imminent, "His Bride has made herself ready" (19:7). Just as today brides wear clothing that has been specially prepared for the occasion, so did those of Biblical times. Psalm 45 is a Messianic psalm. It is in praise of the King and His bride and is fulfilled in Christ and His Church. The bride is shown dressed in glorious garments, leaving her chamber with her bridesmaids to go to the King

(Psa.45:13-14).

Taken in isolation, the words of 19:7 would give the impression that it had been the responsibility of the Church to make herself fit for the occasion. But then it is said, "It was **granted** her to clothe herself with fine linen, bright and pure" (19:8). God made it possible for the "righteous deeds of the saints" to be acceptable to Him. It is the washing of the robes in the blood of the Lamb that makes them white and acceptable at the wedding feast (7:14).

An Invitation

The words that the angel spoke next are evidently especially important. John was told at the beginning of the Revelation that he was to write what he saw (1:11, 19); and to write the words of Christ to the seven churches (2:1, et.al.). Here he was again told to write what the angel said (19:9). It is important because it is about an invitation. The Church is the Bride and there is no doubt that she will be at the marriage supper. But the invitation comes to each individual to accept, and to wash their robe in the blood of the Lamb. It is an invitation for an individual to become a member of the Church, to be included in the marriage celebrations.

The Lord Jesus said that the kingdom of heaven may be compared to a king who gave a wedding feast for his son (Matt.22:1-14). The parable tells how those who had originally been invited refused to come to the feast and even killed those who came with the invitations.

The invitation was extended to any who would listen. Of those who responded, one was thrown out because he had not bothered to put on a wedding garment. Jesus said, "Many are called but few are chosen" (Matt.22:14; Eph.1:4).

It is God who issues the invitation (Rom.8:28-30). To those suffering persecution, it would be a great comfort to be reminded that they are God's specially invited guests.

Worship God

John's response to the angel's message was to fall at his feet to worship him (19:10). The apostle must have been so delighted to hear of the imminent marriage supper, the final vindication of the Church, that he acted spontaneously without thinking. The angel's response was immediate and abrupt: as we might say, "None of that!"

The angel said that he was simply a servant of God just as were John and his fellow Christians. Like them he was engaged in true prophecy which is to tell out "the testimony of Jesus". That is, to proclaim what Jesus said and to bear witness to all that He is and has done.

The Christians in Colossae were being told that if they did not worship angels, they would be disqualified as Christians. Paul said that those who were telling them this were thinking in merely human terms and had abandoned their dependence on Christ (Col.2:18-19).

Angels are far inferior to Jesus the Son, and it is the Father's command that all angels must worship Him (Heb.1:4-6). Angels are "ministering spirits sent out to serve for the sake of those who are to inherit salvation" (Heb.1:14). The angel's advice to John was, "Worship God."

A Celebration of Victory

The prophet Ezekiel was told to prophesy against Gog, described as "the chief prince of Meshech and Tubal" (Ezek.38:2-3), but whose real identity is not known. He is presented as the leader of God's enemies. God will bring them "from the uttermost parts of the earth" (Ezek.38:4-6). He will summon them to a battle (Ezek.38:8) against Israel (Ezek.39:2) in which they will be defeated (Ezek.39:3-5). The prophet was to summon the birds to feast on their dead bodies. God would prepare that feast (Ezek.39:17-20).

This would take place in "the latter years" (Ezek.38:8). The battle and the summons to the feast that John saw and heard (19:17-21) are the fulfilment of that prophecy of Ezekiel.

The subject of John's vision is once again the destruction of human opposition (17:1-19:5). The beast and the false prophet, the secular and religious leaders of mankind organised in opposition to God, are captured and thrown into the lake of fire. All their followers are destroyed.

But the focus has switched from the opposition to the One who carries out God's just judgment. Every statement made about Him is in the present tense. This is what our Saviour is eternally.

Faithful and True

He is faithful and true (19:11). He is absolutely reliable and is not influenced by anything except the truth. He will rule the nations "with a rod of iron" (19:15), with inflexibly righteous justice and in full control.

He makes war in righteousness. He is motivated by the desire for what is right and true. In making war He has no desire to get glory or riches for Himself. He is not vindictive, He wants only what is right and just. It is "the winepress of the fury of the wrath of God the Almighty" that He treads (19:15), without fear or favour.

The Word of God

Greek philosophers had used the expression to refer to the principle that gives order to the universe. Jews had used it as an indirect way of referring to God. They would have considered using His name irreverent.

In view of that, it is not surprising that, in a Church of Jews and Greeks, existing in an empire pervaded by Greek culture and using the Greek language, "the Word of God" was used to express truths about the person of Christ. This is "the name by which He is called" (19:13).

He was in the beginning with God and was God (John 1:1). All things were created through Him (John 1:3; Heb.11:3). He "upholds the universe by the word of His power" (Heb.1:3).

The word of God is powerful (Gen.1:3) and achieves His purposes (Isa.55:10-11). It follows that He defeats His foes "with the breath of His lips" (Isa.11:4), with the sword which comes from His mouth (19:21; cf. Heb.4:12).

All-Powerful

"His eyes are like a flame of fire" (19:12), penetrating to the inner secrets of every heart so that nothing is hidden from Him.

He has a name which only He knows. Every teacher knows that to maintain control over a class it is essential to know the names of the pupils. Knowing the name gives power. But knowing Christ's name, to fully comprehend Him, is beyond mere human intelligence. No-one has power over Him.

It is not clear if "the armies of heaven" (19:14) are Christian believers or angels. What is clear is that they carry no weapons and their robes are not blood-stained. They ride on white horses sharing in His victory. But He does not need their help. He suffered and died alone; it is the sword from *His* mouth that strikes down the nations; *He* will rule with the iron rod; and *He* will tread the winepress of God's wrath.

Victorious

God's King rides on a white horse (19:11), a symbol of victory. John is not shown any details of the battle. It is as if victory was so quick and inevitable for Him that the details are not worth mentioning. Indeed, the victory has already been won at the Cross. "He is clothed in a robe dipped in blood" (19:13), His blood shed at Calvary. The devil is a defeated foe (Heb.2:14).

In the vision the victory is complete and every foe has been destroyed. The emphasis is on "all the birds" and that they were "gorged" with the flesh of the dead (19:21). The image also symbolises that, being deprived of a proper burial, they are disgraced in the eyes of the world. The world sees them for what they really are.

Jesus Christ wears a multi-layered crown (19:12) to declare that His kingdom is without limits (11:15; cf. Isa.9:7). The name on His robe and on His thigh for everyone to see, the name that is no secret, is "King of kings and Lord of lords" (19:16).

11. Thrones and Dominions
Revelation 20:1-15

The different ways of interpreting the thousand years of these verses may be grouped under three headings: premillennialism, postmillennialism and amillennialism. It would require a great deal of space to deal thoroughly with each group. This is because within each group there are different ways of fitting in the predictions of the Gospels and the Epistles.

Whichever explanation is preferred many questions are left unanswered. With this subject especially, there is a need to be sufficiently humble to say that we do not know.

Premillennialism

The basic belief of premillennialism is that Christ will return before the thousand years. Both the sequence of Revelation and the thousand years are interpreted literally. The coming of the rider on the white horse (19:11-21) is the second coming of Christ (1 Thess.4:13-18). "The dead in Christ will rise first", then the whole Church will be caught up to meet Him and join His triumphal procession to earth where Christ and His people will reign together (20:4).

During that time, Satan will be bound (20:1-3). Then he will be released, only to be defeated and thrown into the lake of fire (20:7-10). The final judgment before the great white throne (20:11-15), and the creation of a new heaven and a new earth (21:1) will follow.

Among Premillennialists, the emphasis is often on how, in the last days, attitudes and behaviour will deteriorate (2 Tim.3:1-5). The challenge for every Christian is to keep oneself ready for His coming (Matt.24:45-46).

Postmillennialism

Postmillennialists believe that the thousand years will be a definite period of time in which Satan's activities will be restricted. This will allow the Gospel to be preached throughout the world (Matt.24:14). During that time there will be a great turning to Christ among the Jews (Rom.11:25-26).

It is held that Christ will return (1 Thess.4:13-18) after the millennium. Satan will be released briefly to face final defeat and the lake of fire. The judgment of all before the great white throne (20:11-15), and the creation of a new heaven and a new earth (21:1) will follow.

Postmillennialism was especially popular during the nineteenth century. It was believed that, with the benefits of scientific advances, everything was getting better and better. The growth of the British Empire, and of colonialism in general, meant that the freedom to preach the Gospel throughout the world was increasing. But the "age of gold" that was sung of in the nineteenth century carol faded away and Christ did not return.

Nevertheless, it is held that the Church should be striving towards such an age. The end will not come before the Gospel has been proclaimed throughout the whole world (Matt.24:14).

Amillennialism

In amillennialism it is pointed out that, although there is progress in time in Revelation from the first vision and the letters (1:1-3:22) to the new heaven and new earth (21:1-5), the progress is not in a continuous sequence of events. As has already been suggested, it can be helpful to think of it as climbing a spiral staircase with the scenes visible from windows being shown again but from different perspectives.

For example, immediately before the announcement of the thousand years, there has been a flashback (19:11-21) to the destruction of human opposition (17:1-19:5). Therefore, it does not necessarily mean that the millennium follows the return of Christ.

It is also taken into account that much of Revelation is

symbolic. A literal chain and pit (20:1-3) would not be effective in restraining Satan who is a spirit. It is concluded that the thousand years is probably not to be taken literally.

When Jesus was accused of casting out demons by the power of Satan, He implied that He was able to cast out demons because He had bound "the strong man", Satan (Matt.12:24-29). If this is the binding of Satan referred to in Revelation, then the "thousand years" began with Christ's first coming.

In the Church age, Satan's power has been limited in that the Gospel has been freely preached. "The times of ignorance" (Acts 17:30) caused by "the god of this world" blinding people's minds (2 Cor.4:4) came to an end. The Spirit of truth (John 16:13) is at work in the Church and through the preaching of the Gospel (Acts 19:20).

The time will come when Satan will be released to trouble the earth again (20:7-10) "for a little while" (20:3). He will come in great wrath because he will know that "his time is short" (12:12).

Amillennialism challenges the Church to make the most of these days of opportunity. As the twentieth century song put it, "Now is the time to take the kingdom". The "day of salvation" is now (2 Cor.6:2).

The First Resurrection

Following the sequence of premillennialism, the resurrection of those who had been faithful even to death (20:4) would take place at the Lord's return (1 Thess.4:16). Then the thrones occupied by those with authority to judge would be set up on earth.

However, of the English Versions only the RSV and ESV give a translation that indicates that John is writing about two groups, the martyrs and those who have been completely faithful. The Greek is best translated so that only one group is referred to. In the vision of the second beast it is said that all who refused to worship the image were killed (13:15). The one group in John's vision would then not be "the dead in Christ" of 1 Thessalonians 4 but specifically of those "who had been beheaded", that is the martyrs.

In addition, previously in Revelation when John saw thrones they were in heaven (e.g. 4:4). If that is the case here then the martyrs are seen on thrones in heaven. By their very presence there they are vindicated and, at the same time, condemn those who had murdered them.

This understanding of who it is that are raised and where the thrones are suits both postmillennialism and amillennialism. The first resurrection (20:5) could then be understood in terms of John 11:25 and Ephesians 2:4-5.

Satan's Defeat

On being released, Satan will make one last desperate attempt to destroy the work of God. In fulfilment of the prophecy (Ezek.38-39), he will deceive the nations of the world into thinking that, if they follow him, they will win. He will gain a huge following, "like the sand of the sea" (20:8).

John then switches from recording what he has evidently been told to what he saw. He wrote, "They marched up over the broad plain of the earth." John saw that the armies of the nations were so vast that they were able to attack from all directions and surround God's people.

The people of God are described as "the camp of the saints": they are God's soldiers. They are described as "the beloved city", in contrast to "the great city", Babylon. God's people are those who are submitting to His rule.

The armies summoned up by Satan may be vast but, as in the earlier account (19:19-21), no details of the battle are given. Evidently Satan's defeat is swift and overwhelming. His army is eliminated by fire from heaven (cf. Ezek.38:22). Satan's throne, his power to rule and influence others (2:13; 13:2), is taken from him.

The devil was thrown into the lake of fire to join the beast and the false prophet (19:20). They will be tormented day and night forever (20:10). There will not be one moment's relief from their suffering and it will never end.

The devil had been behind the deceit that the false prophet had practised (13:14). Satan's defeat will bring all deception to an end. From then on only truth will prevail.

Final Judgment

The next scene is awesome. John saw a great white throne. It is white because from it perfectly just judgment will be given.

The presence of the Judge is so terrifying that earth and the heavens fled from Him and "no place was found for them" (20:11): they were destroyed. John does not say who was seated on the throne, but Jesus said that He had sat down with His Father on His throne (3:21). It is "the throne of God and of the Lamb" (22:1). God is the "judge of all the earth" (Gen.18:25; Psa.94:2) but He judges through His Son (Acts 17:31).

John saw the dead standing before the throne. All dead, great and small, whether from the sea or from "Death and Hades". Nobody was exempt.

Even believers will stand there. Paul, when warning against judging one another over differences of opinion about what foods are lawful wrote, "We will all stand before the judgment seat of God" (Rom.14:10), and "each of us will give an account of himself to God" (Rom.14:12). He also wrote that his reason for making it his aim to please God was that "we must all appear before the judgment seat of Christ" (2 Cor.5:9-10).

The difference between believers and unbelievers will be

what is recorded in the books (20:13). Everyone will be judged according to what they have done. Their fate will be determined by where their names are written. Those whose names are not found written in "the book of life" will be thrown into the lake of fire. The lake of fire is "the second death".

Death and Hades will also be thrown into the lake of fire. Death is the normal end of life for everyone. Hades, called Sheol in the Old Testament, is the abode of the dead. Christ has the keys of Death and Hades (1:18). He will set free those subject to death and the fear of it (Heb.2:15) who call upon Him. In the end, Death and Hades will be destroyed altogether.

Comfort for the Suffering Church

It is clear how this chapter would have been of tremendous encouragement to the seven churches and can be to the persecuted Church today.

It gives absolute assurance that Satan's activities are strictly controlled by God (20:1-3). At the same time, it shows that the course of history is in God's hands as He decides on the "thousand years".

Some had lost their lives for the sake of Christ and the Gospel (2:13) and Christ had called them to "be faithful unto death" (2:10). The visions of this chapter give the assurance that those who have been faithful to death are not only with Christ but are reigning with Him. That fact is a clear judgment on their murderers, showing how evil they are.

There is comfort here in that it shows that however powerful their enemies may seem, when the time comes, they will be destroyed in an instant.

At the Great White throne there will be justice for the faithful: eternal torment for their enemies, but vindication and life with their Saviour for them.

It will be worth it all when we see Jesus
Life's trials will seem so small when we see Christ
One smile from His dear face all sorrow will erase
So bravely run the race till we see Christ

So we can confidently say, "The Lord is my helper; I will not fear; what can man do to me?"

(Heb.13:6)

12. For the Glory of God
Revelation 21:1 to 22:21
Everything New

Heaven and earth had fled from the presence of the One who was seated on the great white throne (20:11). In their place John saw a new heaven and a new earth (21:1). This had been promised through Isaiah (Isa.65:17, 66:22).

John does not describe what the new heaven and earth are like, except in one detail. That is that "the sea was no more." Because the sea is untameable it was always seen as being evil or a source of evil (cf. Isa.57:20). For example, in the visions given to him, John saw the first beast rise out of the sea (13:1; cf.Isa.27:1). That source of evil will be done away – there will be no sea.

In that connection it is worth noting that the word for "new" has to do with quality. Peter wrote that the new heaven and earth for which we wait are those "in which righteousness dwells" (2 Pet.3:13).

The making new of all things is so important and fundamental to salvation that God Himself spoke to John about it from the throne (21:5). He repeated the command to John to write it down (cf. 1:11, 19) because what He has said may be relied upon completely. In fact, these things are so certain that God could say, "It is done!" (21:6). He can say this because He is "the Alpha and the Omega", He begins and finishes all things. Whatever He has planned is as good as done.

A Work in Progress

However, God's plan of salvation is a work in progress. God told John, "I *am making* all things new." It is not that God is leaving all His "making new" until the end of time.

When the last trumpet sounds, our bodies will be changed from mortal to immortal in the blink of an eye (1

Cor.15:51-53). However, "our inner self is being renewed day by day" (2 Cor.4:16; cf. Col.3:10). We "are being transformed" into the likeness of Christ "from one degree of glory to another" (2 Cor.3:18).

The same idea is seen in John's description of his vision of the New Jerusalem. The New Jerusalem is "the Bride, the wife of the Lamb" (21:9-10). She is the Church. Twice John tells us what he saw. Each time he wrote that he saw her "coming down out of heaven from God" (21:2, 10). Coming from God she is God's handiwork (cf. Matt.16:18). Coming down, rather than being already down, she is a work in progress. The description of the city being made of gold, and decorated with jewels and with gates of pearls, represents what she will be when the work is finished.

God's Dwelling Place

It was evidently always God's intention to have fellowship with the people He had made (Gen.3:8). Their disobedience spoiled that and they were removed from His presence (Gen.3:23-24). After the Exodus, God began to show His plan for restoring that relationship. Moses had to instruct the people to build God a dwelling place exactly as God showed him (Ex.25:28-29). God said, "My dwelling place shall be with them, and I will be their God, and they shall be my people." (Ex.37:27). When that dwelling place was complete, the glory of God filled it (Ex.40:33-34).

The Israelites departed from God's ways and fell into idolatry. The glory of God left the temple (Ezek.10:18), but the prophet was shown that it would return (Ezek.43:1-2).

The Gospel of Jesus Christ is all about God returning to dwell with man (21:3). The Incarnation was the fulfilment of the prophecy that the virgin would conceive, bear a son and call him Immanuel, "God with us" (Isa.7:14; Matt.1:22-23). In his gospel, John wrote that "the Word became flesh and *dwelt* among us" (John 1:14). "His own people did not receive Him" (John 1:11), but the Church is made up of those who do receive Him (John 1:12). And God dwells in the Church by His Spirit (Eph.2:22).

The Former Things

When God has finished His work, and His indwelling of the Church is perfect (21:3), all the former things will have passed away (21:4). These are the things that belong to the old order that resulted from Adam's sin, in which "sin reigned in death" (Rom.5:21).

Jesus by His death has dealt with sin and has risen again (1 Cor.15:17-20). God gives us the victory over sin and death through our Lord Jesus Christ (1 Cor.15:57). When the last trumpet sounds, the prophecy will be fulfilled, "Death is swallowed up in victory" (Isa.25:8; 1 Cor.15:54). Death and Hades will be thrown into the lake of fire (20:14).

God Himself will dwell among His people and give them His personal attention. "He will wipe away every tear from their eyes." God will remove everything associated with death, the mourning, the crying and the pain, and they will be no more. God's curse that was the result of Adam's sin (Gen.3:17-19), and that falls on all who fail to obey God's law (Gal.3:10), was borne by Christ at the Cross (Gal.3:13). There will no longer be anything accursed (22:3). Citizens of the New Jerusalem will be God's servants, worshipping Him and subject to the rule of God and the Lamb.

The Water of Life

As with so much else in this book, the idea of a life-giving river does not have its origins in Revelation. It goes right back to the Garden of Eden, where the tree of life grew (Gen.2:9-10). It is seen in the account of the time the Israelites were in the wilderness: "they drank from the spiritual Rock which followed them, and the Rock was Christ" (Ex.17:6; Num.20:8;

1 Cor.10:4). The Psalmist described God's blessings as "a river whose streams make glad the city of God" (Psa.46:4). Ezekiel had a vision of a life-giving river flowing out from the temple (Ezek.47:1-12). Zechariah foretold that, on the day of the LORD, living waters would flow out from Jerusalem (Zech.14:8).

The source of living water is God Himself. In his letter to the Corinthians, Paul was claiming that the Israelite's source of water was Christ. Jesus told the Samaritan woman that He would have given her living water (John 4:10). He said that whoever came to Him and believed in Him would have rivers of living water flowing from their hearts (John 7:37-38). John saw the river of the water of life flowing "from the throne of God and of the Lamb" (22:1).

The source of living water is God. This is confirmed beyond question by the fact that, as John explained (John 7:39), living water is the Spirit of God.

Conditions

Certain conditions must be met if anyone is to drink of that living water.

God gives the water of life to those who are thirsty (21:6; Isa.55:1). Without that sense of need, no-one will ever come to Jesus and drink (John 7:37). But to those who come, He gives without payment. The call by the Spirit and the Bride to come (22:17) is followed by the promise that those who are thirsty and really want their thirst quenched may take of the water of life without payment.

Jesus said that whoever believed in Him would receive the living water. Through coming to Christ and believing in Him, one becomes a member of His Church, His Bride, a citizen of the New Jerusalem. That is essential to having access to the water of life because the river of the water of life flows through the city (22:1-2).

It is the one who conquers who receives, as a child

inheriting from its father, the right of access to the source of life (21:7). Conquering means returning to one's first love (2:4-7), remaining faithful through suffering (2:10-11), rejecting false teaching (2:14-17), resisting temptation (2:20-26), keeping the faith (3:3-5), and being genuine (3:15-21).

In contrast, those who do not conquer will suffer "the second death" (21:8). The cowardly are those who put their own safety first. The faithless are those who give way when the going gets tough. The list goes on to include those things against which Christ warned the churches in His letters. It ends with liars: those who act in direct opposition to the Spirit of truth (1 John 4:6).

The Tree of Life

As a result of Adam's sin, he and Eve were driven from Eden so that they would not be able to eat of the tree of life and live forever in their fallen state (Gen.3:22-23). In the vision given to Ezekiel he was told that "on both sides of the river there will grow all kinds of trees for food … their fruit will be for food, and their leaves for healing." (Ezek.47:12).

John was shown the reinstatement of access to the tree of life and the fulfilment of Ezekiel's vision (22:2). Jesus has saved His people from their sins. Angels stand at the gates of the city (21:12) and nothing unclean may enter (21:27; 22:15). But cherubim and flaming sword (Gen.3:24) no longer stand in the way of those who have washed their robes in the blood of the Lamb (22:14; 7:14). The way back to the tree of life is open to them.

"The leaves of the tree were for the healing of the nations." Not only Jews but also Gentiles can believe, enter and be healed. The gates are inscribed with the names of the tribes of Israel (21:12). The foundations bear the names of the twelve apostles (21:14), sent to make disciples of all nations (Matt.28:19). By His blood Christ has "ransomed people for

God from every tribe and language and people and nation" (5:9; Luke 13:28-29). People of all nations will walk in the light of God (21:24; cf. 1 John 1:7), and their rulers will pay homage to Him (21:24, 26; Isa.60).

The Bride

It was one of the angels who had been instrumental in pouring out God's final judgment (15:1) who showed John the city, the New Jerusalem (21:9). It may seem incongruous that the same angel should be involved in two such different tasks, but salvation would be impossible without the destruction of evil. This applies in personal lives also. The reason for John's grief when it seemed that no-one was worthy to open the scroll (5:4), was that he knew that unless evil was destroyed there could be no relief for the suffering Church.

John was shown a city "prepared as a bride adorned for her husband" (21:2). But he was shown a vision of what was beautiful beyond earthly comparison. Try to imagine a city of which even the foundations are built using precious stones! Try to imagine gold like transparent glass or a city gate made of a single pearl! (21:21). For John to get a clear view of heavenly things, it was necessary for him to be taken up into a high mountain (21:10; cf. Mark 9:2-3).

It is impossible to be absolutely certain about the identity of the stones and jewels mentioned here (21:11, 18-20). But the most important thing about the city that John saw was that it had the glory of God (21:11). In Revelation jasper is evidently a symbol of God (4:3). John compared the radiance of the city to a jasper that was as clear as crystal (21:11). He wrote that its wall was built of jasper (21:18) and that the first foundation was jasper (21:19). The city is God's handiwork and He has given it His glory.

The jasper was crystal clear, and the gold was like clear, transparent glass. John saw the Bride of Christ as being absolutely pure. That will be true when God's work is done. It is what every citizen of the New Jerusalem should be striving for (Heb.12:14).

Dimensions

Measuring is a symbol of God's detailed knowledge of His people (2 Tim.2:19) and of His care and protection (2 Pet.2:9). The fact that the measuring rod used by the angel was of gold (21:15) emphasises the importance and value of His people to God.

In the vision, John saw the city as a cube (21:16). The Bride, the Church is the new Most Holy Place (cf. 1 Kings 6:20) in which God dwells. Even when only a few are met together in Jesus' name, He promises that He will be there (Matt.18:20). Such experiences are imperfect, but when God's work is done God's people will enjoy perfect fellowship with Him. There will be no need of "means of grace". The receipt of God's blessings, and the praise and worship of Him will be constant and direct (21:22; 22:3-4; ct. Ex.33:20-23).

Each side of the cube measured 12,000 stadia which equals about 2,500 kilometres. The size is impressive. Symbolically it means that space is not limited, there is room for whoever believes in Christ (John 3:16).

The wall measured "144 cubits by human measurement" (21:17). A human cubit was about half a metre, so the wall measured about 72 metres. If that were to be taken as its height, it would be totally inadequate for a city that was 2,500km high. If it were taken as its thickness, it would be an inadequate footing for a wall that was 2,500km high.

Perhaps this was a wall surrounding the city cube. It may be another way of signifying that access is limited to those who believe, and everything unclean is kept out. The measurement being the square of twelve may be a symbol of it being completely effective.

Uninterrupted Light

There will be no night there (21:25; 22:5). There will be no need of sun or moon or lamp (21:23; 22:5). The glory of God will fill it with light (cf. Ex.40:33-34). The Lamb who is the light of the world (John 8:12) will be its lamp.

For security, the gates of a city would be closed at night. The gates of this city will not be closed by day (21:25) and, since there will be no night, the gates will never be shut. The city will always be open to receive the homage of the nations (21:26) which is God's due.

Jesus at the Centre

This book is "the revelation of Jesus Christ" (1:1). It is all about Him. These chapters are no exception. The Lamb is central to all that is revealed here.

The New Jerusalem is described as the wife of the Lamb (21:9). It is emphasised that the twelve apostles are apostles of the Lamb (21:14). The book of life which has been referred to earlier in this revelation (3:5; 17:8; 20:12; 20:15), is once again clearly named as the Lamb's (13:8; 21:27).

The Lamb is spoken of in ways which put Him on a footing equal to God. The temple of the city, and therefore the centre of worship, is "the Lord God Almighty and the Lamb" (21:22). The city has light because "the glory of God gives it light, and its lamp is the Lamb" (21:23). The throne is twice referred to as "the throne of God and of the Lamb" (22:1, 3).

Finally, Christ takes for Himself the title "the Alpha and Omega" (22:13). At the beginning of this revelation it is applied to "the Lord God" (1:8).

This gives the context to the repeated command of the angel forbidding John from worshipping him (22:8-9; see 19:10). The angel is just a messenger, sent by the Lord God to make this revelation (22:6). Jesus Christ is equal with God.

Trustworthy and True

The words of this prophecy are trustworthy and true because they come from "the faithful witness" (1:5; 3:14), the One who is called "Faithful and True" (19:11). The claim, therefore, applies, not only to the immediate context, but to the whole book.

What He says may be relied upon because He is "the beginning and the end" (22:13). He began everything at creation and will bring everything to the conclusion which He has determined.

His reliability may be checked against the Old Testament record. He is both "the root and the descendant of David" (22:16), fulfilling the Old Testament from beginning to end. But He is not simply another David, or a repeat of some other Old Testament character who failed. He is "the bright morning star" heralding a new dawn and a brand-new era in which there will be no sin and no failure.

It is, therefore, vital to keep what is recorded here (22:7; cf. 1:3). To keep is, of course, not just to remember but to allow what is written to change thinking and behaviour. Blessing from God will result from that.

On the other hand, to add to or to take away from what the Lord Jesus Christ the Son of God has said will have serious consequences (22:18-19).

He is Coming Soon

Three times Jesus says, "I am coming soon" (22:7, 12, 20). This saying also is trustworthy and true. "Soon" is to be understood in the light of the fact that "with the Lord one day is as a thousand years, and a thousand years as one day." (2 Pet.3:8)

Daniel was told to keep secret what he had seen in a vision because it applied to a time in the distant future (Dan.8:26), or to "the time of the end" (Dan.12:4, 9). The end time has come and, because "the time is near", John was told not to seal up this prophecy (22:10).

It must be open to be read and heeded because, when Christ comes, and He is coming soon, He will "repay each one for what he has done" (22:12). Judging by the letters to the seven churches, Christians as well as unbelievers need to take notice of this.

Of course, there will be those who, whatever is said and whatever warnings are given, will persist in living according to their characters (22:11). This verse may also be a warning not to leave repentance too late. Evil, filthy, righteous or holy, all are dependent upon the grace of the Lord Jesus (22:21).

Those who love Him and have put their faith and trust in Him, will respond to His promise that He is coming soon, "Amen. Come Lord Jesus."